100 Skills of the Successful Sales Professional

100 Skills of the Successful Sales Professional

Your Guidebook to Establishing & Elevating Your Career

Alex Dripchak

BUSINESS EXPERT PRESS

Leader in applied, concise business books

100 Skills of the Successful Sales Professional:
Your Guidebook to Establishing & Elevating Your Career

Copyright © Business Expert Press, LLC, 2021.

Cover design by Charlene Kronstedt

Interior design by Exeter Premedia Services Private Ltd., Chennai, India

First published in 2021 by
Business Expert Press, LLC
222 East 46th Street, New York, NY 10017
www.businessexpertpress.com

ISBN-13: 978-1-63742-062-1 (paperback)
ISBN-13: 978-1-63742-063-8 (e-book)

Business Expert Press Business Career Development Collection

Collection ISSN: 2642-2123 (print)
Collection ISSN: 2642-2131 (electronic)

First edition: 2021

10 9 8 7 6 5 4 3 2 1

Description

How many times has someone said to you—oh you need to read (x) to which you provide a cordial lie of "Thanks, I'll check it out!"

Now, for every time that's happened to you, tally on a piece of paper. How many books do you "have to read?" My guess is you said somewhere around 25.

The good thing is this book encapsulates 27 bestselling books on sales and relationship development (many of which are on your "must read" list) and weaves their core messages into my personal viewpoints, anecdotes, and recommendations.

For those who say—that's OK, I like buying many books; terrific! So do I. But here's my second question to you: Of those books you've bought, how many have you read cover to cover? My guess is it's less than 70 percent. Why is this? Books are often long, tedious, and surprisingly repetitive. Through the 215 to 611 word skill sections, there is no droning and rambling on here.

Because we learn best in threes, how about one more reason why to read this book? How many of you are disciples of data? Lovers of lists? Whether it's an article on the 10 best vacations in 2021, the 50 colleges with the best ROI, or the 20 best pizza places in the city—chances are you're more a consumer of Buzzfeed, Thrillist, Vice than you are of personal development books. Let's fuse the style of the two. This book appeals to your innate love for list countdowns (debate away with me @areyouworkforceready on Instagram) and uses the "poised pithiness" and "conscientious candidacy" we love in our daily reads to change the name of the book game.

So, whether you're looking to up your sales game, decide if sales is right for your career, or simply extract some negotiation, persuasion, storytelling, or relationship-building tips to apply to your life—come take a walk on the "wild" side…

Keywords

career development; sales; sales management; business development; relationship building; professional/business; personal development; self-development

Contents

Acknowledgments

First, I would like to note the authors of the books I cited herein this book. You were all my muse to penning this skill development-oriented guide to sales. What started as me looking to sharpen my skills turned into an opportunity for me to highlight my views, anecdotes, and approach in a consolidated countdown. Without your great works, this book would not have happened.

Second, I would like to thank my friends, family, and loved ones for their time, effort, and energy in helping me with their suggestions, revisions, and support throughout the process. I would be remiss if I did not name those who helped me most, so a great deal of gratitude to: Susan Dripchak, Nesha Rosado, Eric Dripchak, Graham Douglas, and David Dripchak for their input and edits along the way in an area (Eric and Graham excluded) beyond their typical interests!

Next, I would like to thank Brian Gore for providing his expertise in reviewing my plan rollout as well as Xavier Roliz and my Commence Cofounder, Tim Denman, for their skillful feedback.

A rather quirky albeit important acknowledgment goes to my Apartment Building, Alta LIC, for allowing me extra time in the lounge to finish my thoughts when in a "writer's flow."

Lastly, I would like to thank all those named or alluded to in this book. You have provided great opportunities for me to learn early on in my career the sales keys to success and are held in high professional esteem.

About Commence

Commence is a revolutionary skill development model born to fix the fact that nothing truly prepares students for the workforce. This college to career individualized coaching program endows students with the power (fka "soft") skills they'll need to safeguard professional, financial and social success. In line with this book, Commence has architected an action-oriented, adaptable playbook for students to learn from and leverage in their life after college. Those interested in enabling and accelerating their workforce readiness can find out more at commenceyourcareer.com

Introduction

For anyone picking up this book who's been in sales, you're asking yourself—what can some 29-year-old kid teach me, about sales? My answer to you… Probably not much. In fact, I'd argue that all the sales gurus out there—Gitomer, Konrath, Iannarino, and so on would say the same. This isn't physics where I'm teaching you some always-true equation. It's not geography where I can say for sure where Timbuktu is. It's in Mali for those picking up their smartphones about to search (one minor step to make your life easier—skill #59 ☺). This is sales. It's where you take creative ideas, processes, where-you-stand methodologies, questions, scenarios, and so on, and tailor them to your individual client situations to create an ever-evolving playbook so you can adapt quickly to changing needs, decision makers, business climates, and more.

What I've done in the chapters to follow is take the myriad of best/next practices from the most lauded sales geniuses as well as from my experiences in consulting and tech environments and make a different kind of playbook out of it all. After reading 27 of the best sales, relationship-building, negotiation, and presentation skill books, I've compiled, vetted, and ranked a list of the skills one needs to be successful in finding, developing, and nurturing complex, long-term successful business relationships.

In a society where we love lists, I'm surprised there hasn't been an extensive publishing of the skills you'll need out there in the real world of "make one false move and you're dead" sales relationships.

For those of you that are experienced in sales, you know that sales is almost equal parts "What to Do" as "What not to Do." This book seeks to showcase that fine balance of navigating the minefield of meeting advances, sidesteps, and traps.

For my readers who are coming out of college—especially those in my academy—don't be deterred by a whole bunch of names you don't recognize and seemingly insurmountable odds of winning business. This isn't the embodiment of the cagey, old man cynic saying to stay far away and run to the hills of investment banking or finance. Frankly, we have enough of those. They were your elite business school professors. If you're considering embarking on a journey into the sales profession, you're the ideal reader. This list of 100 key skills will give you a great foundation of what you'll need to be successful. If riding the resiliency rollercoaster isn't for you, there's no shame in going elsewhere! Not even into aforementioned investment banking; great field where hard work is rewarded highly.

In short, for my sales professionals: read to brush up on your skills, especially those in the top 20 and do the action item callouts.

For my students and those soon to be turning the tassel, focus your time on what the skill is, your connection to it, and the feeling you get when reading. Did you finish this book in 2 weeks? Great, exploring a sales career may be for you. Did you limp to the finish line scanning sections and not thinking about it during your days? At least now you know what you don't want to do.

To further refine your postgraduation plans, I'm including a five-step guide (next) from Commence, our Workforce Preparatory Academy, to help you battle test your chosen or anticipated career path.

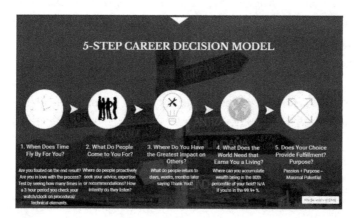

Now, just like you would for any important meeting, let's set the agenda:

1. Read this book noting that every skill is important, but those most critical to winning large pieces of business are those toward the top.
2. Take notes in the margins or separately. There will be 100 actions items and just as many mentions of other important books for further learning on the topic. I'll help at the end with my ranking of the best books to read (top 10 in my order of priority).
3. Pick no more than five skills you want to focus on this upcoming quarter (students, that's 3 months) for your business development efforts. While it's easy to dig yourself into trying to work on all 100, you know where moving the needle will make the biggest difference for your pursuits.
4. Enjoy. Yes, I did list this as an agenda item because it's often hard to do with any book (no one single book I agree with entirely even though Lee Salz's *Sales Differentiation* comes close) and certainly no list. Read with an open mind that ranking anything is subjective. If you think #17 should be #47? Semantics. Don't get bogged down in them. Spend your time in the details of your prospect's business ☺.

For Those of you looking to drill a specific skillset, I've created this categorical guide to further streamline your learning and application of the book:

Individual preparation (17 Skills)	Relation- ship- building (17)	Meeting effective- ness (28)	Mindset and strategy (20)	Negotiation/ persuasion (9)	Internal develop- ment (10)
3	2	1	4	17	9
8	7	5	12	18	48
16	10	6	15	28	53
23	11	19	30	37	60
33	13	20	34	41	67
36	14	24	35	79	69

Individual preparation (17 Skills)	Relation- ship- building (17)	Meeting effective- ness (28)	Mindset and strategy (20)	Negotiation/ persuasion (9)	Internal develop- ment (10)
45	16	25	39	81	84
50	21	26	40	89	93
56	22	27	42	94	95
72	38	29	64		97
74	43	31	65		
80	57	32	66		
90	59	44	70		
91	68	46	71		
92	77	47	73		
99	86	49	75		
100	88	51	78		
		52	82		
		54	96		
		55	98		
		58			
		61			
		62			
		63			
		76			
		79			
		83			
		85			
		87			

CHAPTER 1

100 to 91: Ensuring They Don't Pull the Proverbial "Trigger"

Chapters are General Themes to Indicate Shifting a Prospect's Mindset and not all skills will fall under each general theme.

100. Projects an Attractive Appearance (3 minutes)

Through the eyes of my pen, I can see almost a universal eye roll. "How is that a skill?" Bear with me. In a world where all potential buyers are suspect of sales people from their conjured images of used car salesmen, telemarketers, spam messages from overseas, and so on, you're lumped in. I don't care if you're the top salesperson at SalesForce, Oracle, Microsoft, and so forth—you're in there. Actually you may be Suspect #1. Given your success they will treat you like a hypnotist—I'm not going to fall for her magic spell! No magic wand (or for *Get Out* fans—teacup) can lure me in!

Why all this babble about skepticism? It starts within that five seconds they walk from the door to the waiting room to greet you:

Does this person look trustworthy? Do they look like me? Are they interested in our business or making another sale?

Lauded psychologist Robert Cialdini in his *book Influence: Science & Practice* talks extensively about how those who are attractive make 12 percent to 14 percent more than their counterparts. While there isn't a ton you can do to change your face, skin, or height, there are important touches you can make to connect.

For men I'd say this is a nice jacket, jeans or slacks, a proper dress shoe (moderate shine), subtle smile, and firm handshake. More reader headshakes, I can feel it. You're thinking—suits! I want to show them I take them seriously and look my absolute best! Truth is, suits, unless they're becoming of the environment you're entering (banking, securities, government), are a hindrance. Something we are comfortable with. We as salespeople correlate suits to success.

Going to a meeting? Put on the suit. Going to a conference? Put on the suit! We somehow think we go from Clark Kent to Superman when going into our little telephone booth (bathrooms or bedrooms) and donning the outdated.

Daniel Pink in his *To Sell Is Human* goes into detail about the negativity people associate with salespeople being draped in suits, smiles, and shiny shoes.

In a way **suits are a conformity**. Most sales personnel go suit and tie and what happens? Everyone looks the same. Let me share a story with you and valuable lesson I learned from an....outspoken... CFO.

I was going to meet a new CFO stepping into a Top 10 disruptive company. I tried hard to decipher his style premeeting. His pictures online are in suit and tie. He's an executive, but it's a disruptive company. My final nail in the coffin? Well, this is in Manhattan—NYC is fancy. I'll go suit and drop the tie. Perfect middle ground right? Wrong.

While in the waiting room I realized just how off I was wearing a custom shirt and cufflinks, pocket square, and all. To dress it down, I unbuttoned my top button and lost the pocket square. In walks the CFO and his first words?

"We don't wear suits here in Start-Up World."

I might have well just walked out right then and there because after that it was all skepticism, all mindless tests focused on getting me to stumble rather than explore a potential partnership together.

Action Item: If it's a first meeting, ask about attire in advance. It may sound elementary but it's dually recognized and appreciated.

99. Tracks Client Reference Win Percent (2 minutes)

Ok, so now we made a big shift here from #100 being about mirroring/matching/connecting with your clients initially to how you effectively manage client relationships to win future business.

This point, originally brought to my attention by Lee Salz in his *Sales Differentiation* masterpiece, speaks to the very analytical elements sales personnel must master. In a world where it's increasingly easy to mute, block, disregard, or otherwise eliminate unwanted noise, you need to deliver value quickly. We have **shifted from quantity to quality** in our outreaches. You can't wear people down quite as much these days and that calls out the need to analyze what works. Let's take references as an example. Utilizing client references usually comes at the end stages of a deal or the closing stages of an RFP (Request for Proposal).

We list three references and ask to see which they want to speak to.

While you could win or lose for a variety of reasons, references are a big portion. If you're winning at a tremendous rate and find out it's because they spoke to Jackie @ABC Client, well then Jackie is no longer a *client*, she's an *advocate*. A darn good one at that. Not only will Jackie be your go-to person next time, she should also see an uptick in event invitations, freebies, and anything else to ensure she receives the attention she deserves.

In one step you not only figured out your best "Down the Funnel Advancement" strategy, but also figured out your highest retention priorities.

Action Item: Go through your last five deals: Who did you list as references? Who did they speak to? What percent of the time did you win with *X* contact versus your average or company average conversion rate?

98. Leverages Sales Tools (2 minutes)

Living in a modern, computer-focused, tech-enabled world, it's hard to believe sales tools would rank so low. The reason? It's often outside your hands to make these types of purchasing decisions. Good news? There is a process to buying software or subscriptions and nearly all vendors recognize that. So sign up for the demo!

As opposed to spending 300 words on why they are important, I'll call out my five most essential sales tools to try. I recommend Stu Heinecke's book *How to Get a Meeting with Anyone* for a more complete listing.

Bombora: Intent tracking platform that gives you the ability to see which topics are trending weekly at your prospects.

Discover.Org (now combined with Zoom Info): The mecca for contact information and intelligence on what projects prospects are looking into for those companies partaking in Qualtrics surveys.

Google Alerts (and RSS Feeds): Free! Great way to get the latest news articles involving your selected prospects as opposed to constantly (and sporadically) looking yourself.

LinkedIn Sales Navigator: The Digital Resume provider brings identification tools (who's following your company) in addition to a communications platform (Inmail).

American Cities Business Journals: Not one I'm leveraging today but the same idea applies as the INC 5000 or other lists; what awards and news articles are surrounding your prospects?

Action Item: Sign up for Bombora's free trial and **Take the luck out of timing**! This tool is beneficial for what to say and when to say it. For those managing big territories with deep toolsets, this is a must-have solution and the trial is very helpful in setting up your prospecting outreach.

Follow 10 companies on Google alerts! Be diligent about the exact wording you choose to follow—too generic and there will be tons of results; too specific and you may miss important articles. Piece of advice: For law firms and others written up on advising their clients, manage how often you're getting updates or perhaps choose other companies to follow and lighten your e-mail overload.

97. Monitors Internal Position Constantly (2 minutes)

Some of you are thinking, what the hell is he talking about? Good, I've captured your attention. As author Mike Weinberg says, "sales is a verb" and as such it's constantly changing. What works to what companies and what types of executives—it's all dynamic.

Considering such, we need to change as well. What may have been an active pursuit maybe needs to be moved after your key contact left and put back at the top of the funnel. Perhaps they had a negative experience with another line of business at your company and now are less of the excited internal advocates they used to be so you move back on the Miller Heiman emotion continuum.

If you constantly evaluate where you stand, you will be more in tune with what your clients are thinking, less ready to log into your CRM, and do the "three-month push" of your close date. If you're thinking that doesn't apply and believe your slow-to-sign deal hasn't had changes, you're wrong. Your job is to check with your internal team and cross line of business resources, coaches, and so on to see what may have developed/digressed and how you can handle it.

This not only matters for the deal itself but matters for how you handle your pipeline and, better yet, your territory. If things are retreating back to Identify or Active Pursuit from your Best Few or Committed stages, then you need reinforcements. Adopt the visual from the movie *The Patriot.*

One of the greatest scenes comes from when the Colonials retreat. The Redcoats follow them over the hill expecting to crush them but are instead crushed by the reinforcements the Colonials fell back to. Think of this as an analogy to your struggle as a sales rep: The Redcoats are your Quota; the retreating Colonials, your active, struggling deals; and finally the reinforcements your Pursuits and Identified Opportunities. If you're not advancing ahead, it's time to send in even more reinforcements than you would normally. This not only gives you more irons in the fire, but **changes your emotional state from pressured to poised.**

Action Item: Use the Miller Heiman emotion continuum on key deals to test your gut (show your work). Evaluate every one-fourth of your average deal cycle. This means if your average deal cycle is eight months, you should have a check-in every two months to monitor its progress. Recognize that not all hours are created equal. An hour prepping a finalist meeting is vitally more important than an hour responding to an RFI. Focus and allocate time accordingly.

96. Communicates Efficiently (Count Down, Not Up) (1 minute)

Time is money. For CEOs, asking for 30 minutes is often asking some-one to invest 4 to 5 figures with you. As such, you should be living by the less-is-more principle. Don't waste any words—whether in e-mails, presentations, speeches, and so on. Think about how you can maximize your, and more importantly, their time.

Woodrow Wilson, when asked how long he needs to prepare a speech, famously remarked,

> It depends. If I am to speak ten minutes, I need a week for preparation; if fifteen minutes, three days; if half an hour, two days; if an hour, I am ready now.

Don't think of time as something you fill, think of it as something you **maximize by refining down**. To not be a hypocrite, let's intentionally leave the rest of this page blank and skip to the action item.

Action Item: I'm sure you have a strong one-minute pitch but do your-self a favor and write a three-minute pitch. Now whittle that down to 1 minute, 45 seconds, 30, 15, then 100 words, 25, 10, 1. Deploy as you see accordingly to match your prospect/client's style.

Shift Selling's Craig Elias says you should be able to deliver your value proposition or as Weinberg calls it your "Power Statement" in seven words or less. Can you?

95. Informs and Includes Internal Team (2 minutes)

Sure this one is a little low on the totem pole at number 95 but that's because it's incorporated into many other items. However, this is a book about reminders, tips, action items, and—more than anything—accountability/fastidiousness to strategic and tactical details. Therefore, it gets its own number.

More than anything this is important because it includes another brain to help you solve challenges. I don't care if you've tried "everything"; you don't know everything so chances are you may have missed something plausible. Even if you dotted every t and crossed every I, perhaps someone has the one word to revise your sentiment that will help. (Also perhaps you read something so quickly that your brain told you it was correct—like my prior sentence—and someone else will catch it for you.)

I find that including your internal team does two things remarkably well: It builds your personal brand and it **lessens the resistance** you'll encounter from other team members. Since you probably know what I mean by building your brand (and if not, we have a section coming up on it), let me first address what I mean when I say it lessens resistance. In many consulting/brokerage environments, you have two groups of people: the consultants and then the account management/business development/sales personnel. Like most of the world (outside the 11 percent of people who have sales as their vocation) these consultants probably have a jaded view of what you do. Here's the picture they paint: something along the lines of a smooth-talking, minimal-working, self-serving, not-so-intelligent guy (or gal) who sits over there. Sound familiar? People make shortcuts in their mind and since this is a prevailing stereotype, it's one that even some fairly close colleagues may think.

When you include your team in your pursuits, strategies, psychoanalysis of the buyer, and preparation for every hypothetical situation, they begin to foster a new appreciation of your skills and recognize your value. Once you have obtained a title of "valuable," watch how much more they are willing to do and learn from you.

Given the perception that salespeople are often separate from finance, operations, consultants, and so on (even though we perhaps go across all businesses more than anyone else), there is a thought that you work alone and at times that presents many challenges. When you keep your team up to speed and foster collaboration, they get a rush from the pursuit that will propel your team to new heights.

Action Item: Point out the good and the bad to your team. Sometimes leading with the bad (if delivered with the proper mindset) gets them to open their eyes (oh, you're actually considering the impact this has on me? Or, wow, so you don't just chase every opportunity to sell something?) and gives you an instant ally.

94. Maintains Emotional Consistency (Waiting Room to Elevator) (2 minutes)

It's not rocket science to know that people, never mind buyers, are skeptical of salespeople. I've even had friends think I was sugarcoating something or not being real with them because I'm a silver-tongued salesman, the loquacious life-long peddler.

In a world where people have more access and more reasons to distrust you, the most important items are credibility, trust, empathy, and genuinity (how is this not a word?). Ok so I spoiled the countdown a tad, but on this point of emotional consistency, be authentic.

Some of you may be thinking, but I get genuinely excited to see my clients and prospects I've developed a relationship with, so naturally my mood will shift. My advice? Carry that positivity in when you enter their building. For first-time meetings, this skill is especially important. Think of the feeling you'd have if you spot a salesperson in your waiting room looking kind of sullen or mad staring at their phone then all of a sudden you walk in and now they have a big smile on their face. How do you feel in this scenario? Skeptical at best I'd imagine. You feel a bit used and are thinking, "I'm a potential paycheck to them."

If putting on a happy face isn't something for you, that's also fine. Maintaining balance is important. Whatever your personality is, **commit to it when entering the building**. If you forget to do that, commit to it when getting off the elevator on their floor.

Now on the flip side: Meeting is over, it went well or horribly, and you and your colleagues shake their hands, exchange pleasantries, and head into the elevator. It's not time to berate or celebrate. You don't know who's listening and if you're saying bad things, perhaps you won't hear from them again. If you're overly confident and planning several next steps, someone could hear and tip off your client to let them know they have leverage (price discounts, contract terms, other concessions). Don't let your premature celebration, or discussion, cost you dollars on your deals.

Action Item: Talk to the receptionist. Read their materials. When in the waiting room, read their flyers, books, magazines. Find artwork, sculptures, awards, and so on that are on display—see how you can compliment (not flatter), or connect to, their company.

93. Builds Their Brand (2 minutes)

In order to build credibility and establish yourself as not just another product-pushing peddler, you need to take actions to build your brand. This goes beyond going around the office and making conversation so people know who you are. Sure that's a great start but in order to build a brand and not just inhabit a role and parrot what's on your business card, it takes a lot.

In order to expedite the whole time factor, I'd recommend joining many groups, some virtual but many in person. Chambers of Commerce, Business Journals, position-based groups (i.e., CFOs) are some places to look into in person. Online, I like commenting on shared articles from client's LinkedIn profiles; it shows I'm taking an interest in them, engaging in open conversation on the insights they shared and on a relatively unsaturated medium. Being able to **proactively provide insights/commentary disarms people** while showing you're here to look out for their best interests. Also, when opportunities do arise and they aren't yours, your colleagues and management chain will take notice. With how collaborative selling efforts are these days, there may even be a revenue share/split in it for you.

Be less concerned about your target list and proverbial "bag" and more focused on getting out there and helping people.

Action Item: Start your own website. Sharing featured content in your industry is appreciated. Make sure to balance your third-party data with company-sourced and more tips and tricks from your experience. I find writing quick action-oriented list-style articles (i.e., The 5 Ways to Turn HR into a Profit Center) to be the best balance as showcasing intellectual capital without worrying: Am I sharing too much of my own company's data? If I share my competitor's data will I be driving business for them?

92. Arranges the Day the Night Before (3 minutes)

This was a simple one I learned early in my career and admittedly lost touch with. Let me know if this sounds familiar:

You wake up in a good mood, get into the office listening to your favorite inspirational music and set out to crush your prospecting. You sit there looking at your list of 20 to 2,000 companies and begin reading your old notes: Ok, that one I spoke to two weeks ago and they are busy with Open Enrollment. That one isn't really a good candidate for X. Eh, John hasn't picked up or responded to my 10 messages.

Before you know it, an hour has passed and your inbox is filling up. You get sidetracked, come back to your goal (because you as a reader of this book are dedicated) of crushing your prospecting but based on time and dwindling optimism, you reset your goal of say 30 prospecting messages to 15. Soon enough it's 10. You rationalize to yourself saying, "I mean, it's still double digits and 80 percent of our team isn't doing anything proactive anyhow." Boom 11 messages! Look at that, I overachieved my goal.

Hopefully, a few of you are also laughing at this depiction. While it may be a funny/relatable image it's one we need to change.

When working at Oracle we used to have Century Days: 100 outbound e-mails or calls to prospects with incentives, a leaderboard, and pizza to spur along the intra-squad competition. The key to hitting your 100 effectively and not just phoning in your phone calls (Mike Weinberg—I too enjoy this pun) was planning in advance. A list of contacts, their company, their role, a couple of key recent pieces of news and a general understanding of their business, phone number/e-mail address, and your topic, and you're good to go.

Getting in a flow is critical in prospecting. Too often there's a long lag between picking up the phone or your new e-mail window. It's not something we necessarily want to do and therefore it gets dragged out because realistically it's a 90- or 120-minute block for most of you reading, as opposed to a whole day and it's about getting to the end.

Ok early worms, why do I argue evening before versus morning of? After-hours has a different mental feel—it's extra time where you're being proactive, whereas early mornings, while still fantastic, are the kick-start to your day. You're just beginning and if you're enthusiastic, you're likely eager to get going. That eagerness could cause you to unknowingly cut a few corners you wouldn't the night before.

Bottom line: Planning TOMORROW's work is more strategic than planning today's.

Action Item: Put together a list, I recommend a calendar invitation to yourself with 6 to 10 key, proactive items of importance you want to accomplish the next day. Scale up as needed. The key word here is proactive. Putting down respond to Client ABC in the morning does not make it. Face it, you were going to do that anyway. Don't cherry pick, cheat, or otherwise cut yourself short.

91. Loves List Making (2 minutes)

For anyone who knows me, you're laughing to yourself and then scratching your head saying, #91 Alex?!? That's so low for you!

While yes, I am a personal fan of all types of ranked lists (cocktail bars, world cities, NFL's best wide receivers, steakhouses...) this is something that has served me well in Sales.

It's no secret that time is our most precious asset and that not all accounts are created equally. If that's so, why do you treat them as such with your one master list in Excel and your generic Salesforce dashboard?

Noted Sales author and trainer Anthony Iannarino in his book *Eat Their Lunch* recommends categorizing your accounts much like an Olympics metal podium: Gold, Silver, Bronze. This way you have at least three sections of differentiation.

If you doubt the value of this bringing you more revenue; you're entitled to your opinion. However, what you cannot deny is it will **greatly behoove you in your interactions with your management team**. Having answers to your target list, penetration, total addressable market (TAM), account segmentation—these are the items that instill confidence for your management team.

I'd also recommend knowing your accounts by revenue, employees, installs, in the funnel, touchpoint breakthrough and conversion rates. Being an analytical machine all stems from the fact you love to make lists. So in three words:

Segment. Rank. Prioritize.

Action Item: Create a five-pronged account segmentation list utilizing at least two criteria for how you segmented (size, TAM, employees, current offering, etc.). I'd recommend Diamond, Gold, Silver, Bronze, Copper because it has a common understanding of value and is almost universally known in descending order of importance.

For anyone focused on their QBR (new readers, that stands for quarterly business review) right now, shoot me a note on some of the custom KPIs I've developed in the past that have impressed my management teams.

CHAPTER 2

90 to 81: Getting Them to Lower the Gun

90. Employs Prediligence (Formatting, Calling, Agenda-Setting in Advance) (2 minutes)

For my *Anchorman* fans, I'm envisioning a number of you in your best Champ Kind southern drawl saying, "What-n-the-hell is Prediligence?" To me, diligence is the work we do to be prepared in the meeting. Prediligence would, therefore, be everything we do in advance to ensure not only is the meeting well positioned, but that the meeting actually (drum roll…) happens!

Novel idea I know, but I, for one, am guilty of not employing prediligence several times. Are you?

Well let's see, **did you send over an agenda** for that prospect meeting ahead of time? Did you confirm with a phone call that your conference attendee was still coming? Did you check the bottom right corner to see your page numbers progressed accordingly? I'm guessing you answered No to one of these questions. If you've never fallen victim to any of these—congratulations! You may pass #90 and go straight to #89. Collect $200 in additional commissions.

Let's start with the big ticket item, agenda-setting. Paraphrasing Mike Weinberg in his bestselling *New Sales. Simplified:* agenda-setting is critical because it also keeps us in control of the conversation and helps us navigate the ship's course: identifying and exploring a mutually beneficial partnership. My recommendation, no matter how basic the meeting, outline 3 to 5 topics/items you will cover in your next meeting. Seek their feedback, so this remains a democratic encounter and not an authoritarian interrogation.

Next, checking in with clients. This is perhaps one of the only times to use the universally unpleasant phrase of "checking in." In this sense, it's less "Big Brother Here, Are You Coming" and more "hey, I understand schedules can change last minute, just wanted to see if you're still able to join us." This is a delicate topic, so make sure your outreach is friendly, conversational, understanding, and displays genuine excitement. If you're not excited to see them there, don't say you are. Then, it's a trite, meaningless sales vernacular you're employing that they will spot when they see you and your lackluster energy.

Lastly, for now, are your t's dotted and your I's crossed? Apparently not because that was just written backward; how many of you caught it? Better yet, how many of you remember this was a trick from skill #95?

It's so easy to get in the flow of using templates and replacing the old prospect with the new one. But, did your page numbering go smoothly? Did you control-find to make sure all abbreviations, acronyms, and shorthand names of Old Prospect are gone? They may be minor, but when they rear their head in a meeting, it's sloppy, and the best we can utter is a shameful "Sorry about that."

Action Items? See above. ☺

One more I'd suggest is less problem prevention and more sales differentiation. Take notes from the prior meeting, encapsulate the message, and send it out. It gives you a working document that ensures you heard them right and showcases your listening skills.

89. Writes Well (2 minutes)

When people ask me my major in school, I used to try and cover up the fact that it was English. I would emphasize my "unofficial concentration" in Marketing and my minor in Philosophy. At first, it was shock, then it was unwelcomed surprise; a raised eyebrow if you will. Nowadays, from the best business people I know, it's a reply of "that makes sense" (not knowing which major/minor they are referring to), "English majors have a great hold on how to communicate well."

Not only was it the validation of the incredibly expensive education, it was true! (OK, yes, I'm a bit biased, but hear me out.) The best writers are often the most avid readers. What do you do as an English major? You read. A lot. And, what do you study? Forms of effective communication in long and short formats. What does that help with? Speeches, presentations, conversations, and so on.

With e-mail being the overwhelming selection for **preferred medium of communication**, this is not a skill you can forego; it's a necessity. The introduction, build up, wrap up, and closure usually all happen via e-mail. Of course, the culmination is often in person, but do you have an in-person meeting for every stage of the process? Of course not. Finding a mutually agreeable time on someone's calendar is oftentimes more difficult than the client's personality or the questions themselves!

Careful word selections and confident tone are two pieces of writing you must have in order to be successful in getting meetings and getting selected. And guess what? When it comes time to negotiations, it's also a great time to be a wordsmith for protecting your value and creatively employing contingencies to meet the client in the middle.

The business world is a deliberately delivered dance, and your keyboard is the dance floor—get acquainted with it well.

Action Item: Trying writing some articles on LinkedIn; this is a 2 for 1 special, as it will help boost your credibility while honing your writing skills. The potential win–win–win, for those Michael Scott School of Hard Knocksians, is it may spark a creative prospecting campaign or a potential event to host.

Be concise! Choosing the right words is almost as important as knowing which words to avoid (coming soon!). In today's world of seven second attention spans, think creatively about every word you choose, especially those in your e-mail heading. If you're having trouble being concise, use your signature to be a great repository of credentials.

88. Offers/Gives Items of Value (2 minutes)

Let's face it, no matter how great a blanket item is, it doesn't hold universal value even if it is nearly universally applicable (Amazon gift card).

If you have something that holds unique value, do your homework to see who it would most apply to. Sure the Ohio State Michigan game is fun to see as a general spectator, but who are your fans? Alums? Former players?

Inviting the right subset of people is the difference between thanks that was fun and I really appreciate you taking me, this means the world to me.

If your company allows it, invest the ticket in your top prospect *and* their family member/friend. Giving someone two tickets will make an even bigger impact.

Remember, these events are mainly to showcase your ability to connect, build rapport, showcase your ability to give, and so on. I'd avoid bringing up your company, but you can subtly maneuver onto topics where they may organically bring it up. Keyword there is organic. If they feel it is forced, you are now on the precipice of losing their attention and, more concerning, their trust.

So far, these examples have been on the rather… grandiose side. Football games, tickets, and so on have a distinct allure, but how about for the 363 days of the year you don't have exciting events to leverage? Just because I said value doesn't mean the value on the sticker needs to be high—the value to the person is what matters.

One of my best customers shared (back when she was a prospective client) with me she had recently been on her honeymoon to Hawaii. For most people, this is an excellent conversation, a couple of good e-mails, perhaps even some long-term recollections, but rarely is it more than that. As opposed to the standard fruit or cookie platter for Christmas, she got a wooden picture frame with the name of the island she traveled to.

The picture frame did more than evoke a genuine thank you; it left a lasting impression that working with me features a profound **attention to detail that originates from my deep, personal sense of caring**. And that's exactly what you're gifts should do.

Action Item: What do your prospects truly care about? I imagine you'll really only know this answer for about 5 to 10 percent of your prospects, so make it focused and targeted; you'll go much further hitting home in a big way with few than a mediocre gesture to many.

Be mindful of gift limitations. Most industries, it's $25 per person, but government can be as low as $10. Don't break the limits.

Take notes about your prospects' interests; if they have a dog, find out what breed and perhaps get a calendar for them for Christmas.

87. Doesn't Leave Things Open for Interpretation (2 minutes)

This one comes from Lee Salz's masterpiece—*Sales Differentiation*—and it really hit me. Having worked for the most widely used, enterprise HCM software solution and the perennial #1 HR consulting firm with the most # of clients and market leverage, I was not attuned to how these things standing on their own could be interpreted negatively. We as salespeople think the truth is self-evident: We know you best because we've done it before. Your size, your industry, your competitor—they use us. And here are all of our awards to show it.

The downside? When you say largest, they could think slowest. When you touch on the number of customers, they may think lack of attention.

While some of these traps you may be avoiding already, the one I continue to struggle with is, how do you balance the number of innovative/creative/next/best practices with instilling confidence that they don't have to change much?

Author Tom Searcy of *RFPs Suck!* and sales guru Jill Konrath in her book *SNAP Selling* both talk about how to get your potential clients comfortable with the idea that many things can stay the same; we aren't a replacement—a complete overhaul of the current regime—we are a complement to your current process. As Jill would say, we are "Business Improvement Specialists," not {Transformation Agents.}

So, what's a quick remedy? Explain why a stat, award, recognition, and so on is important. Even if you think it's dumb to do, it can be valuable, and there's only upside. Focus less on explaining why a stat matters—that may be self-evident. Instead take the contrarian, devil's advocate viewpoint, and address it head on!

Example? We are the largest broker with over 3,900 clients; 1,400 more than the next closest broker. Some of you right now may be thinking "Overworked, won't get much attention, small fish in a self-admittedly giant pond." Not the case at all. In fact, we have measures in place to ensure we do not have lead consultants working on more than nine clients considerably less than the majority of other players in the space.

Action Items: Think of the superlatives and recognitions your company uses. Write down the 10 most common. Explore any negatives you can think of from the Eeyore, Negative Nancy, skeptic perspective. Now state your case and **incorporate the implied objection** into your reply.

For example: We are proud to be the broker to over 3,500 organizations, but what we are really proud of is how we've been able to scale up while ensuring our consultants never have more than nine clients to tend to.

86. Plants an Idea Inside the Prospect (2 minutes)

One of the commonalities I see separating small-minded and grand think-ers is small-minded thinkers have an obsession with credit; the small-minded people need credit for everything, while those who think big aren't afraid of their ideas being mistaken as others' ideas. Small-minded people will get caught up in the petty and, much to their own dismay, see a wonderful idea fail in achieving reach and maximal impact.

Now, you may be surprised to hear this, but it's quite simple—your big thinkers are action oriented. They are thinking: I don't care who car-ries the torch as long as we march forward as opposed to: it's my way or the highway.

If you're less focused on credit and more on getting buy-in, you'll go fur-ther in your career. After all, the *greatest form of flattery is through imitation*, so if your idea gets reused by someone else, it's the ultimate compliment.

When it comes to sales, you may be the wordsmith, creative genius at the top of your field, but **you're not always the ideal messenger**. Your word carries more weight if your coach or internal client champion carries the torch for you.

Think of it this way, if it's their idea, it means it's their credit, their raise, and their promotion. If you're the bug in their ear, guess who's coming to the top with them? You. Their success means you've got a client for life, and the greater their success, the more hoops they will jump through and rivers they will cross to ensure you come along as their partner of choice.

If done well, this skill can propel you straight to the top.

Action Item: What ideas and analyses could you be lending your buyers? What's the best time for them? Performance review? Board meeting? Job interview? Leverage these opportunities to go the extra mile for them, and it will pay back in spades.

85. Has a Healthy Appreciation of Relativity (2 minutes)

Oftentimes colleagues, managers, consultants, friends, and so on come up to me shocked they didn't win an opportunity; we were the best! We had the highest ROI! Our relationship was so strong! Take your pick, I hear it often. What I don't often hear is how people compare their solution to what the client needs and what they have used in the past.

You may say, well, Alex, this is a time of transformation, they should be going for the big ticket right away! It saves them from switching down the road. The problem is, most people don't think that far ahead.

If you're a guy, let's take dress shirts for example. At 19, you're probably taking your dad's or brother's shirts for a job interview. At 22, you're going to Macy's. Why aren't you going to Thomas Pink or Bonobos? You know you'll need top-quality clothing down the road. The reason? Because things are relative. Most often people make relative improvements, and this extends into the professional world too.

If someone is riding a bike, the 2000 Honda Civic is fantastic. Sure it may not have Harmon Kardon surround sound or heated seats, but it's a step up. After they outgrow the Civic, then it might be time for a trip to your Lexus dealership.

Moral of the story: If they are spending 20K today and your solution is $100K, you may want to focus your time somewhere else because no matter what you say, 98 percent of the time, they have been **"Getting By"** at one-fifth the cost.

Action Item: Look at your most recent wins; how did their prior vendor compare to you on functionality, price, and service? Take an honest assessment. Compare this assessment to your prior wins to see what your market premium is (the amount they paid more for a similar scope at your competition). This will give you a general idea of your ideal target client.

84. Rehearses (2 minutes)

Perhaps the simplest skill, but also one of the most vital, is rehearsal. Your challenge? Getting others to buy into the idea. Many may think rehearsal and overkill are synonymous. At my own company, I hear either "I have *X* years of experience" or "I know what I'm doing"; all leading to "I don't need to rehearse."

For anyone else who has a significant gap in age between yourself and your team, this is a tough one to deal with. However, it's vital you persist. Weddings have rehearsals—you agreed to those. I think if you can stomach the mindless 30 minutes at your buddy's rehearsal wedding, you can stomach an hour rehearsal to win a significant piece of business and either lay the foundation to, or further cement, a client relationship.

This one is especially ironic because 9 times out 10, you will discover something critical that was left unturned beforehand. Whether it's:

✓ If you checked with their A/V team about setup
✓ Asked about attire for the meeting
✓ Finished name tent cards
✓ Confirmed the number of printouts
✓ Established who is going to begin introductions
✓ Determined who will summarize and ask for action items

There are a plethora of details that go unknown into the rehearsal.

If you get significant pushback, reference these factors and have them think of it more as a **"Walkthrough."** For whatever reason, people relax and agree to walkthroughs versus rehearsals. Perhaps, it's the light-nature of the word "walk." After all, it isn't a sprint through, and it isn't a traverse through; it's just a walk. Slow and steady. John with 30 years of experience can appreciate that.

One important item here: Get someone or some others who can sit in and play the client. Preferably, this is someone who is familiar with what you do, but not all the intricacies. This will ensure you communicate clearly and explain things in a way an educated, yet not expert, person can keep engaged.

Action Item: Block out time for a walkthrough for your next finalist meeting. Do it in person! Think of who serves a similar role to your buyer. Consider personality types, relevant pet peeves, styles, and so on. Invite these people ahead of time. Be considerate—no one wants to be roped into your roleplay last second.

83. Elicits Thoughtful Replies (2 minutes)

One of the overarching principles of the sales masterpiece *The Challenger Sale* is to get your client/prospect thinking, "Huh, I never thought about it that way before."[1] In meetings, I oftentimes see people asking the layup questions. How many employees, what states, which systems—salespeople are very comfortable and very good at getting baseline information from clients and missing opportunities to really peel back the onion.

As legendary speaker and author Simon Sinek would say, **get at the Why**.

Why are you now unhappy with the status quo? Why did they consider your company? Why not their incumbent advisor? The "what's" and "how's" can be important for the baseline, but eventually, we need to hit a few 3s to win the customer's mindshare. You aren't going to elicit thoughtful replies from asking "what" questions. Bridge questions like "Have you considered?" Powerful points of view—"Why" questions—will.

Now some of you may already be asking these questions but not allowing time for replies. We as salespeople believe that silence will lead into, "Well, thanks for coming in today". The worst nightmare. The nemesis to discovery meetings—the lead-out before you even had a chance to really get rolling.

Don't panic. Give your clients a second to think. If they have paused, they are taking your question seriously, and they are, secretly, impressed by your ability to help them see another way. Pausing is different than shifting. If your client starts gesturing to their distant notebook, briefcase, watch, then these may be signs to consider what powerful question or transition you have to leverage in your Hail Mary. But, give it time. Filling space not only eliminates their ability to think, it ruins your chances to connect. To be memorable. To showcase your suave. Yes, you read that correctly. Consider this: babbling on shows a lack of confidence, and that's an unattractive display of gripping on too tight.

Action Item: Practice your pauses. Roleplay and have your manager, colleague, or friend test you. When you're babbling on and not pausing, have them call you on it. As you get better at being flagged immediately, have your friends start blowing their silent whistle—keeping track mentally and letting you know afterward where you may have missed the mark.

82. Knows the Solutions Well, More Than What's Expected (2 minutes)

Like it or not, salespeople are often viewed as the superfluous and unavoidable middlemen. When you couple that with the fact that many of us work for middlemen-type companies (brokers, intermediaries, etc.), it makes working with us all the more difficult in the eyes of the client. Clients will try and go around you to work directly with consultants. They will look for shortcuts to solutions. Most of all, they will try to minimize the level of detail they go into with you as they think you'll need to, or worse off, they will need to, parrot everything back to those actually completing the work.

Sound familiar? It's happened to all of us, and it's one of those things—like stubbing your toe—that never seems to hurt any less the more it happens. Of course, I could throw some generic language at you about the importance of being credible and valuable, but without real-world applications sprinkled in, it's not all that helpful. So, here goes:

Know your solutions well—better than the rest of your sales team or the baseline/certificate of completion level. When you're able to know your solutions, how they compare to others in the market, the process it takes to evaluate a potential fit, and so on—you make yourself credible right from the beginning. All prospects go in with a skeptical mindset about their account manager (sales person), so knowing your solutions, company, and process well goes a long way in changing their mindset and putting stock in valuing your relationship.

Anthony Iannarino in his book *Eat Their Lunch* talks about the concept of a **52 percent SME**, meaning to know 52 percent of what your subject matter experts (SMEs) would know. I love the concept and think it should be used as a barometer of when you are field sales-ready. We all have that uncomfortable feeling of, "when am I ready?" when you start a new job, and 52 percent SME is a good starting point.

If you can answer just over half their questions, you're good to get out there and start trying because you'll keep ticking that number up the more opportunities you get. Also, 52 percent will soon become 65 percent after your first dozen meetings or so. Before you know it, you'll be up to

80 percent of the way there if you're an active listener, note taker, reviewer, and analyst of what's been working.

The 52 percent SME is a great way to build credibility, as it enables you to respond quicker to clients (with answers), which in turn makes you more autonomous; a great way to build credibility within your company as well.

Action Item: Listen in on first meetings, discovery calls and demos to see what questions come up, and how many you would have been able to give strong answers to. Review the answers provided by the SMEs to see what you can learn and incorporate into your repertoire.

81. Focuses on the Right Information (2 minutes)

Can I ask you a personal question? How many deals have you won with just one buyer? What percentage of your total deals is that? As I can't hear you, I'm going to venture a guess that it's not many. Despite this pedestrian realization, I oftentimes see, and become the victim of, short-sighted, singularly threaded opportunities. We as salespeople don't want to jump over our point of contact who feels more like a friend (even if they don't think so) than a buyer.

In today's day and age, where experts estimate that the average deal involves just under seven decision makers, we as salespeople often think and act on the fact that 1 strong VP-level contact or higher is enough.

This is just one example of how **we can become a horse with blinders on**. Now I'll agree with Miller Heiman training that sales is a side-sport like swimming or running where you're racing side by side toward a shared interest (as opposed to a face-sport like boxing), but running straight ahead and running straight ahead without peripheral vision is a distinguishment I'd make. (Yes, I created a word just now.)

It's vital to constantly reassess your position (as I'll discuss later on), but it's also important to have a guiding framework foundational to your success, and that starts with focusing on the right information. No two deals will be exactly the same, but just because you have a really strong relationship with a prospect (unless it's your parent), it doesn't mean you get to ignore other indicators like approval layers, ratifiers, budget, budget timing, and so on.

Within each opportunity, you should assess all buying powers and players, competitors, alternatives to your solution, priorities, timing, indicators (like responsiveness), fit, and current state. Running through these eight areas (and more) will give you a foundational look into the totality of your opportunity.

Action Item: Evaluate your wins. Now evaluate your losses. Where were your differences? What key information did you not have in advance for your losses? Make that a vital category of importance for your opportunity scoring rubric. Review your rubric and each category weighting to see where your winning scores are. The lowest number is now your new threshold in establishing and advancing your pipeline/funnel.

CHAPTER 3

80 to 71:
Establishing a Basis

80. Manages Appropriate Expectations and Overdelivers (2 minutes)

If there is one key to business, I would say it is the following lesson:

Do your best to *underpromise and overdeliver.*

This lesson is closely tied to managing appropriate expectations and setting the right precedent. Responding to clients within 5 minutes is fantastic, but if you do it all the time, it becomes the expectation. The moment you respond 25 minutes later (which by all measures is still fantastic), you'll find they are more annoyed at how long it took, as opposed to pleased by how much quicker you are than everyone else.

If it's something you can control, **keep your SLAs** (service level agreements)/KPIs (key performance indicators) **on the low end of your actual range.** If you expect an answer by noon from your internal team, say you'll get back to the client by the end of the day. Don't unnecessarily put yourself on such a tight schedule as you never know when you may run into an issue. And, if you don't? Well you just overdelivered. Another benefit? People either think you are very efficient or you pushed the envelope to make them a Priority 1. Either way, it's a win–win. Or, in the Michael Scott School of Business, a win–win–win (in this case, because I win for helping you with your clients).

One of the most important areas to underpromise is in your prospecting. It may sound counterintuitive, but it's important for two critical reasons.

First, it isn't a one-size-fits-all approach. You understand what you offer (unless you literally give money away to people for nothing), solve problems, and some people may not be experiencing the problem you solve. A great way to begin a conversation is to talk about assessing a fit. Now, this turn of phrase is fairly overused, so if you're trying hard to impress your client with how upfront you are, say you'll collaborate with your team to see if it makes sense for YOU—client *XYZ*—to consider your company's solutions.

Second, even if you can solve this challenge 99 percent of the time, you don't want to promise a Yes and push for how great your solution is in this area if that 1 percent actually does raise its head. This happened to me once early in my career and no matter how many other skills you implore after this, you're pretty much on the backburner... permanently. If you're like me with a tool chest of 80+ solutions, you'd hate for 1 tool to ruin your chances of fixing the client's leaky foundation.

Action Item: Look at the promises you are extending now; are you on time? Are you late? How often are you early? See how you can finish early more often.

79. Is (Subtly) Persuasive (2 minutes)

One of the biggest misconceptions I come across is that so many people think sales is solely about persuasion; like you're some kind of sorcerer or hypnotist altering people's states to get them to buy from you. Not at all.

When you pick up any book on sales, chances are you won't find a one liner or sequence of phrases strung together that will wind-sprint you from the bottom of the stack rank to the top. Instead, it's about managing the entire process. Jeb Blount reiterates this constantly in his book _Inked_ and Lee Salz talks about the need to differentiate consistently within each step of the sales process in his book _Sales Differentiation_. Sales is a marathon, not a sprint (not even a wind-sprint), and if you try and make it one, you'll do more harm than good.

Today's buyers are smart, and they know when someone is trying to pull a fast one on them. Years ago, salespeople held a lot more of the cards and did a lot more informing (price, terms, common practices, etc.). Today's day and age is more about sales professionals curating content and making the experience easier than it is about teaching information.

You may help interpret information but you won't be viewed as the sole source of data, so don't try and act like you are. There's no quicker way to burn a bridge than to try and take a shortcut like assuming your buyer is ignorant and inept of finding the right information. Tactics like glide-handing, preemptive closing or trite, overused slick phrases are other sure-fire ways to set your career on fire (and not in the inspiring way).

In short, this skill is more of a don't than a do. In the few cases where you do need to get someone off the fence, move with concerted confidence. Taking options off the table, reassuring them that you're not going anywhere, or finding other ways to showcase leverage will work in your favor more times than not.

What I'd recommend when you are looking to get someone on your side is to **utilize another voice that isn't your own.** Ideally, this would be a happy current customer, but if not, an industry expert, past client, team member, and so on will also do the job as their voice carries more weight than yours. Remember, at the end of the day, you do profit from a sale and they know that, so when you need to get creative in persuasion, be delicate, transparent, and quiet.

Action Item: How can you build your persuasion skills through enabling others to speak on your behalf? Where can you be so confident that you can walk away convincingly?

78. Earns the Right to Give Advice (2 minutes)

One of the hardest grounds to test is to understand when someone expects you to offer advice and when it comes across as presumptuous. Its difficulty and accompanying murky waters make it number 78 on this list.

In sales in 2021, you have to be well researched, creative, and bold. Oftentimes, many people mistake that with offering unsolicited advice, so let me help you distinguish the difference. Let's take a look at two outreaches to the same person.

> Hi Joann, congratulations on making INC's fastest growing companies list; that's no easy feat for anyone, never mind someone in the Utilities space. Despite adding over 100 employees in the last year, I noticed you were still receiving applications via e-mail; I think you should implement an Applicant Tracking System to help automate your recruiting process and ensure you maximize your productivity while beginning a smooth onboarding process for your top talent and capturing tax credits. When do you have 10 minutes to discuss next Wednesday or Friday?

Versus

> Hi Joann, congratulations on making INC's fastest growing companies list; that's no easy feat for anyone, never mind someone in the Utilities space. Despite adding over 100 employees in the last year, I noticed you were still receiving applications via e-mail; have you considered an Applicant Tracking System? We are seeing a number of utilities organizations similar to you implementing them to help maximize staff productivity and capture eligible tax credits. **Is this a priority for** you? If so, let me know when your schedule permits a 10 minute conversation next Wednesday or Friday.

The content is virtually the same, but in the first case, I inserted my opinion/my advice even though it wasn't asked for and certainly hasn't been earned. You can have a point of view, and you can offer industry/competitor trends, but be careful of how you come across. Smart and considerate is a lot better than ignorant and arrogant.

Action Item: Ask your manager or team member to have a look at your prospecting note and ask them if the tone is appropriate. Consider lightening your perspective and tone by asking questions like: Does that resonate with you? Would you like our/my advice? Would you like to know what we are recommending to clients in your situation?

77. Consistently Delivers and Returns Quick, Quality Replies (2 minutes)

There are a few contenders for easiest to accomplish on this list, and let's just say this one is up there for most uncontested layup. Don't believe me?

Think of your best internal resources, what do they all have in common? They get you answers… quickly.

Returning messages quickly not only shows that you consider them important, it helps expedite sales cycles. Now, I'm not saying to drop everything to respond to your prospects. After all, if not done correctly, this comes into direct opposition with mastering the art of not caring; a skill we will discuss later on.

My advice on how to walk the tightrope? Have your **messages look more like read receipts** than formal replies. If you think you're toeing the water of desperate, talk a step back and send one liners about how you'll look into this and have already sent it to X resource. Even better? Do it from your phone and leave the little "I'm busy and important" message that reads: Sent from my iPhone.

Really concerned you're doing too much, too quick? Put up your Out of Office or, if that's not something you're comfortable with, a note that says how you're in various meetings throughout the day and will do your best to return their message as quickly as possible. It's accurate, it conveys what you want, and it starts triggering your prospective client's mind that you and your company are doing well (better come aboard before prices go up!).

Action Item: This one is really up to you as it is stylistic. You could mark messages you haven't responded to as unread or use other ways to flag or categorize.

I think a good practice to get into is to go through your e-mails at the traditional close of business (5, 5:30, 6) and send your replies either later that night or scheduled for next day. Don't be afraid to use Delay Delivery in Outlook!

76. Effectively Manages Gaps in Communication (2 minutes)

Lending you some counterintuitive thinking: once someone is interested, avoid following up. Sounds crazy right? Well, it isn't as crazy as the news headline sounds; let me expand. Avoid following up about *that project too quickly*. They didn't forget about your project and definitely don't need a babysitter.

Now let's not get carried away and think this means the end to our engagement with them. Instead you should find ways to **engage them on parallel streets** (well-being seminar as a parallel for a benefits brokerage deal). These streets get you to have your prospect continue down the road of relationship-building without feeling forced to gun it at the yellow light. The best part? The roads converge just a few minutes away.

Some ways to continue staying in front of them without being forceful include sending invites and evites to webinars, seminars, conferences, even some happy hours or appropriate special events.

Now that you know what to do, a piece of advice: pick your spots. Don't send something because it's on your to-do calendar today and you'd like to feel accomplished moving that item to the completed tasks list. If there's an event coming up in 3 days, hold off on the webinar perhaps. Or if that event would be much more attractive with their peer (your client) attending, get your client to RSVP first and use it as leverage and momentum.

For those of you wondering "When do I worry they aren't interested? 2 days with no response? 5? 10?" Here's my rule of thumb (take it with a large grain of salt): 2 weeks. If you had something out there and haven't heard a single word for 2 weeks, it's time to get creative. Now if someone gets back to you, unprompted, at 2 weeks and a day, take that as a good sign. While they may have just missed the window, they spent the time to either flag/save your message and mark it on their calendar to reply or they spent their valuable time to dig it out of their inbox.

Action Item: Write down what means you have to engage effectively when you're already acquainted. Client holiday party? Baseball tickets? Upcoming conference (with free pass?)? Correlated vendor/partner introduction? Keep these items in mind by writing them down in a place you frequently check.

75. Employs Creative Tenacity (2 minutes)

"We're measuring your job performance."

Figure 1.1 Redefining the Measuring Stick of Performance: Effectiveness > Quantity

For all of you writing this one down thinking, "what a marvelous turn of phrase," I can't take the credit. In fact, it was from my first sales director at Oracle. Cool phrase, but what does it really mean?

It means finding new and innovative ways to stay in front of a prospect or customer. Not "just checking in" and not a perpetual lunch invitation.

If the definition of insanity is doing the same thing over and over again and expecting different results, why do we as sales people so often relent into this pattern?

Well, it starts with our days being divided and our need to rationalize anything as being productive. After all, 20 messages that took 5 minutes each is a heck of a lot better than 5 messages that took 20 minutes each, right? Unfortunately, this is how many of us (myself included) think. Worse yet, it's how many of us are incentivized; especially those in inside sales!

To help minimize your time wracking your brain for ideas (and falling further behind on your call quotas), I've included some examples of creative tenacity. Stu Heinecke, in his book *How to Get a Meeting with*

Anyone, has a number of great ideas (some seen next), but some of my personal favorites over the years are also listed:

- ✓ **Wedding invitations** between the marriage of your two companies, their two divisions, and so on.
  - ○ Credit to my former colleague Nick Gregoretti.
- ✓ Magic 8 ball—will *X* respond to my message? Today, my 8 ball said yes.
- ✓ Gradual campaigns—sending one card at a time; building a royal flush.
- ✓ Handwritten cards.
- ✓ Floral arrangements (ensures it gets delivered straight to their office).
- ✓ Preprogrammed phones with a call when it is delivered.
- ✓ Cartoons (Stu Heinecke himself).
- ✓ Messages in alternate/native language of the buyer.
- ✓ Items of personal value (step beyond geographic interest and into something compelling).
- ✓ Resume of your company's skills to be a fit for the company (yours truly).

Action Item: Read *Thinkertoys* by Michael Michalko and study his action-oriented approaches to being creative like "Getting Tone" and "Don't be a "Duke of Habit." These easy changes to make will open up your world in ways you didn't expect.

74. Recognizes Non-Buying Signs and Words (2 minutes)

Most people do not consider sales to be a job of vetting. They really just think of it as a job of getting (lucky). Truth of the matter is, you need to be diligent about what you spend your time pursuing. Just because someone is interested in your business doesn't mean you should be jumping through hoops to get their business.

The best place to be diligent is in an RFP. Why? Well, for starters, it's because it is a labor-intensive process and also it either: favors the incumbent (right-hand man advisor) or the lowest-priced solution.

Tom Searcy in his book *RFPs Suck!* does a fantastic job at explaining all the signs to look for, but one of my favorite sections talks about identifying passive interest and how words like "consider," "perhaps," "explore," are all words that should leave you concerned. If something seems generic, off, or thrown together—it's not you, it's them. And it's telling you to close the file.

In general, these things on their own are all caution signs or as Mahan Khalsa would say, Yellow Lights. As Khalsa discusses in his book *Let's Get Real or Let's Not Play*, you want to **move warning signs to go/no go** as quickly as possible and to employ a series of well-thought-out, perspective-taking, frank questions to do so.

What warning signs and weak language/format have in common is they all point to discrepancies in your ideal customer. Whenever I discuss ideal customer profiles, people typically mention their customer's employee population, revenue bands, location, or industry—the demographics.

What they often miss is the opportunity to segment on psychographics. Psychographics are the attitudes, emotions, and fundamental values of an organization. Like:

★ How quickly do they adopt innovation?
★ Do they value quality over quantity/lowest price?
★ How paternalistic are they?

The answers to these questions may be even more important than your demographic fits depending on your line of work.

Other nonbuying signs to be wary of?

- Abrupt endings to conversations
- People being overly agreeable or polite
- Consistent/constant rescheduling
- No incentives/measurements driving the point of contact forward

These characteristics are sure to sideline/delay deals, and delayed deals are one of the toughest parts of sales. If you can minimize those, you free up time, build credibility with your management team, and make for more accurate forecasting.

Action Item: Write down five psychographics that are vital to how your clients think versus how your stalled or lost pursuits have thought. Where are the stark differences? How can you better prepare to address those items?

Bonus! Action: Give people actual green, yellow, red lights to ensure you're hitting on their needs in real time (Mahan Khalsa's idea).

73. Is Empathetic (2 minutes)

As I write this book, I realize there are a number of skills I'd attribute to doctors or psychologists as something they do better than the traditional sales person, but it manifests itself just as much, if not more, in business development than it does in the medical field. What is it? Empathy.

People go to doctors for intermittent chest pain, they see psychologists for painful memories that took place 10 years ago, but yet somehow their troubles at work on a daily basis go without professional help.

Now empathy is not something you can learn from an expert, but it is something you can improve. In fact, this is the one "skill" or rather indicator of personal character I'd say that can dramatically compensate for shortcomings in other areas. I've actually had some really strong sales people ask me a question about a pain point, and when I reply that it is a challenge, they go—"Great! We can fix that for you." Now, I'm a rather understanding person, but when I hear their enthusiasm, I think to myself—no. No it's not great that my life has been miserable for 8 to 12 hours a day for the last 3 weeks you self-serving jackass.

It's gotten to the point where I think a positive interaction with a salesperson means they don't shoot themselves in the foot with their inability to connect through empathy. I just write it off that neutral means positive; imagine what actual empathy can do for you.

Empathy to me starts with body gestures. Nervous laughter about a prospect's issue is not your time to join in laughing nervously, it's your time to stand out by taking a pensive pause for something troublesome, leaning in and asking a powerful and poignant question centered on them, recognizing alleviation for this pain (and not something centered on your company solving the pain).

Empathy, like many things, is a fine line to walk in sales. It's important to balance your empathy with your ability to challenge your prospects. By challenge, I don't mean aggressively disagree, I mean point out potential issues or repercussions from missing something. As Deb Calvert points out in her book *Discover Questions*, "It's those who call your attention to potentially hazardous situations"[1] that are the people you trust in your personal life.

Connecting with empathy in a self-centered and surface-level world is a great way to gain trust at the beginning of a new relationship, and being brave enough to note a potential issue is the way to cement a cultivated connection as a relationship centered on trust. Be empathetic about the items that benefit you and the ones that don't (not making a change, needing to wait, project not being a good fit for the client). Don't just use empathy when it benefits you.

Action Item: Video record a practice intro meeting—are your actions and body language/gestures consistent with empathy?

72. Observes and Notates Client Engagement (2 minutes)

Daniel Negreanu. Phil Ivey. Phil Helmuth. Three Great Poker players and most likely three people NOT at your presentation/negotiation table. While many procurement and CxOs may laud themselves as negotiation experts, there is one area they (or their colleagues) fall amazingly short—putting on a poker face.

While the old statement about 93 percent of communication is nonverbal may be flawed, it still holds a lot of value. Someone twiddling their thumbs, on their computer, or avoiding eye contact is either not listening at all or has something to hide. Actions speak louder than words, and body language is an action. If someone says that everything is clear as a bell and terrific but didn't listen to a word you just said, that's because you're not at the partner evaluation table, you're at the process-box-checking table.

On the flip side of the coin (or in this case, playing cards), there are little signs to look for when a client is happy. One is **the inclusive "we."** Jill Konrath in her book *SNAP Selling* talks about how if you hear your client saying "We" (When do we get started, When we work together, How would we do X) and "When" in lieu of "If" are subtle word choices with markedly unsubtle impact to your deal pipeline.

One sign that I was the welcomed recipient of? The double handshake. We went through and shook hands with everyone at the end of a finalist presentation and what happened? They shook our hands again and walked us out. I told the team we were their preferred choice. What happened? We won.

On the other side, when escorted out at a different recent meeting, the client moved toward the lunch room instead of toward the door to continue talking to us. Why? Their "job" was done, and that's all it was. Fulfilling a task, not exploring a partnership. Haven't heard on that one and not holding my breath.

What's the importance of all this? Write it down! These are some of the first things we may miss or forget about days, weeks, or months later. When reviewing something purely on its merits and logic, you'll miss these amiss body gestures.

Some of you may be thinking, what should I look for? Well, for any fellow poetry lovers, it's much of the same. Look for repetition (what do they keep coming back to?), pitch (did their voice break somewhere? Why?), emphasis "Did they emphasize the price? The time? The approval process?" And, all other forms of poetic devices.

Well, maybe not iambic pentameter—as impressive as that would be.

Action Item: Mood map! Just as Dan Pink recommends in *To Sell is Human*, on a scale of 1 to 10, how engaged and interested in you/your team were they at the beginning? Middle? Immediately after key information presented (price, timeline, any nos., case studies)? At the end?

71. Mitigates Fear, Insecurity, and Attachment (2 minutes)

Thinkertoys by Michael Michalko is often commended as the premier book on creativity, and while I appreciate its ingenuity and ability to get you to think outside the box, I was impressed by something Michalko had to say that has nothing to do with creativity.

Prescott Lecky, a self-image psychologist, helped a salesperson become successful without changing his work ethic, network, or prospecting efforts. He drew a simple picture: *You wouldn't get down on all fours like a pig in front of your prospect, so why do you do it mentally?*

His lesson was one I think resonates with every single salesperson out there: not to be overly concerned about whether or not your prospect will approve of you. Fear of not being liked, aka insecurity, begets obsequiousness, and obsequiousness translates to weakness; for in your kissing ass, you're showcasing you are not to be respected, and how can you be trusted if you are not first respected?

Any mobster, gang member, or otherwise power movie seems to always feature a self-assured protagonist whose no-nonsense attitude wins them respect. While I don't think modeling gangbanger mentalities is a guidebook to sales success, it's a lesson in how (perhaps) we should exercise a little less caution and be more ready to share our point of view.

Fear and insecurity are two of Jeb Blount's seven disruptive emotions from his negotiation book, *Inked*. A powerful third to keep an eye on? You guessed it—attachment. As Blount says "attachment is the enemy of self-awareness and the genesis of delusion."[2] I understand the feeling salespeople get when they are working in complex or enterprise-level selling situations; you've worked on something for close to a year, so you desperately (another deadly sales sin) work to keep it alive. You're the 5-year-old who can't give up your blankie, and unfortunately for you, the blankie has plenty of germs on it to hold you back and keep you down.

All three of these sales sins have something in common: they are focused on you viewing potential failure as the worst thing that can happen rather than success being the light to your career. When you're focused on what a positive situation looks like you can harbor those behaviors and be ready to **forego justifying holding out hope for a negative situation to get better.**

Action Item: Where are fear, insecurity, and attachment present in your deals? How can you correct them? How have you overcome these difficulties to win deals in the past?

CHAPTER 4

70 to 61:
Building a Relationship

70. Is Upfront, Candid, Direct & Honest
(2 minutes)

Some of you may be reading this thinking—"those 4 words go together, why separate them out?" Here's why: they all build credibility.

I think when we say these words, we reassure ourselves that we are doing all four of these. But when you think of how long business meetings are and how much of a discussion is organic/impromptu, you can realize… maybe not all the time.

Being upfront captures people's attention, especially those particularly distrusting or skeptical of what you have to say. One of my favorite examples of addressing skepticism is from Adam Grant's book *Originals* where he notes how you can take ammunition out of a cynic's gun by leading with the five reasons not to do business with your company. If one of the five issues is a deal-breaker, you can be on your merry way. If not, they can relax and listen with a sound ear, appreciative of your candor.

Being candid also can do you a lot of good. One word to the wise—don't use the phrase "honestly or to be honest" because, what were you doing otherwise? It's a phrase of poor terminology, especially in the sales world. Replace it with "Frankly."

Being direct means answering questions simply. Concisely. People don't like beating around the bush and even if your answer is completely transparent but long, people may get the wrong impression.

Lastly, honesty goes a long way. Saying "I don't know but I know someone who may" is proactive and helpful. Doing your follow-up looks more put together than answering on the spot. Think of a doctor who says they are going to consult with others or check research—don't you feel more confident after they deliver validated information?

Action Item: Think of where you can **flip the script and cut to the chase**. Even if it's a minor area, point out where a competitor has the same capabilities. Point out certain areas being not as important, even boring perhaps. Tailor the severity of your words to your audience, but look to capture attention 2 to 3 times per presentation with something upfront, candid, direct, or totally transparent.

69. Identifies Total Addressable Market and Builds Go to Market (2 minutes)

Some of you may be reading this and thinking—that's marketing's job. Well, reality check time.

Marketing materials are usually flawed and don't take your client base into account. Pie-in-the-sky—generic is the best way to characterize the materials that often come out, and sometimes, that's enough, but many times it is not. Make these materials your own. Make them tailored to your client. If someone sees you took something boilerplate and made it about them, they will appreciate it.

Total addressable market (TAM) is not only a stat your management team has or will ask for, but it's also a way to stay optimistic about your territory. When you have 50 accounts, 10 are installs, 7 are wed to competitors and 15 are impossible to reach; it's easy to lose hope quickly. When you break out the dollar figures your prospects' represent in each line of business or solution area, the **sheer size will get you motivated again**.

While it's ultimately a motivating activity; make it realistic. List the qualifiers (aka limitations) of TAM. Do you seldom steal business from one competitor? Don't include that prospect in your TAM and call out why. Was someone a prior client and had a vociferous departure from you? Well, until the old regime leaves, that one should be factored into a lower TAM as well.

Other items to consider for making your TAM as tam-gibile as possible, include factoring in if a company has:

- Declared bankruptcy
- Been acquired/divested
- Had a recent organizational change or hardship
- Notified your company that you do not qualify as a supplier
- Overlapping competitive offerings
- Partnership with your competitor
- Prerequisite purchases (first need an Applicant Tracking Software before an automated tax credit)
- Foreign parent (buying authority)

Action Item: Build one model for a go-to market and then tweak and tailor it to suit your other lines of business, solutions, or verticals. Many of the items you need to capture will overlap across the board, so be thorough in your first go-round.

68. Offers Input About Client's Competition (2 minutes)

One area that your client lives, eats, and breathes (unless they are in Higher Ed, the land of the all-welcoming) is their competition. Whether it's competing for donations, dollars, or donuts, they, like you, have competitors. So, what do you know about them? Chances are probably not much.

I think you should fix that.

If someone is behind the curve—they need to play catch up. If someone is knocking it out of the park, they want to keep the fans coming back. Either way, it's an opportunity for you to succeed. Oftentimes, just mentioning their competitors (or as we fancy consultants say, peer group) gets their ears to perk up; much like a dog when you ask if he/she wants to go for a WaLk? Well now that you and man's best friend are curled up reading this section, let's continue:

Read and set up Google Alerts for your clients and their key 3 to 5 competitors. What's coming up in the news? What headlines relate to your work? Now don't stop there. Headlines are great, but what if your client hasn't read it yet? What if there's a curveball in there you didn't see coming? Don't come this far just to fall short. It's like running a marathon and stopping at the last mile.

Discussing your clients' competitors also shows that you are a proactive thinker. You're looking around the turn to not only see what they should be doing, but who else is doing it, how are they doing it and what are the implications of implementing this action. **People like consultants who can connect the dots**—in fact it was the #1 need one of my recent clients told us they needed in a new consultant.

Lastly, discussing their competition shows you care. You aren't babbling on about how great you are (effectively mitigating your self-oriented needs), and it keeps them talking, which, nearly everyone with a mouth likes to do. You can't track every single prospect's competitors, and they know this. The fact you've gone above and beyond for them showcases not only your drive but your prioritization of time and placement of time on them.

Action Item: Now don't think you can pull some caffeine-inspired, all-nighters and track every client's competition; be diligent about your top prospects. For those of you handling a universe greater than 150 prospect accounts, let's say your top 5 to 10 percent of accounts.

67. Identifies and Enables Useful Partnerships (2 minutes)

The best way to prospect for potential business is to leverage credible client connections and voices to do your bidding for you. A motivated advocate that's genuine is hard to duplicate. Pending that you've already *tried* that route (or more like are *trying* to develop), the second best route is to enable useful partnerships. Sounds about as generic as possible, so let me define that a bit further. Look into the areas that are correlated to, similar to, focused on, or peripheral to, your products and client base.

Let's take the example of health and benefits brokerage services. My correlated area would be benefits administration software; it's something people need in order to carry out the activity we are discussing. What's similar to benefits brokerage would be 401k brokerage: serving similar buyers for a similar service. For "focused on," let's assume I specialize in assisting professional services firms. In this case, getting to know a professional services automation (PSA) software provider would be beneficial.

Lastly, for areas that are in the periphery of my client's focus, I'd partner with them too. In the world of health and benefits, well-being providers are becoming more and more a topic of conversation. They, like many of my other partners, have sales goals, and those sales goals involve companies and buyers similar to mine. Sometimes, it's easier to kill two birds with one stone for you, your partner and for the client juggling their calendar and trying to fit you both in separately currently.

One of the other best ways to prospect is to offer your company as a client; if you have the brand name or size where it might actually make sense. Exploring organizational synergies and opportunities to best serve our shared client bases by learning each other's offerings are great ways to showcase how you're an outside-the-box thinker who is dedicated to his/her craft.

If you're not getting through to your buyers or their executive team, try reaching out to their business development (commonly abbreviated BD) team; this showcases your ability to put their end goals ahead of your own and the word, especially a successful word, travels not only fast but high up the food chain.

Action Item: Find five companies you can help outside of selling your solutions. Ask yourself, "Are you a potential buyer of their solutions? Do you have a partner who could be partner to them?" Perhaps, you have a client you can introduce to them or at least **pursue business jointly as a united front.**

66. Is Calendar Flexible (3 minutes)

A wise philosopher once said, "You only get one shot, do not miss your chance to blow, this opportunity comes once in a lifetime." For those of you too old, or scarily enough, too young, to get this reference, it's no philosopher—it's early 2000s rap sensation Eminem.

This is a particularly powerful string of lyrics for any salesperson, as it's quite true. And while we may not be doctors on call to save lives, we are on call. As I'm writing this, I'm thinking about how to respond to my brother asking me to get together tomorrow (New Year's lull week) with the question, "Are you working?" Well, that depends. It depends on whether or not this client decides they want to finalize negotiations. If not, I'm free for the golf simulator and lunch. If so, sorry bro (literally), I'm getting called in.

Some of you may be cringing right now thinking when you're out of the office, you're out. Some may advise you against what I'm about to say but my advice is: You should (almost) always be partially available. Why? Being hard to reach is the easiest way for someone to justify not tackling a problem or working with your company.

Plus, nothing says I'm committed like taking a call on a day off and nothing says I love my job quite like dialing up the VPN from some exotic destination and... looking forward to it!

This one goes hand in hand with being in love with your career; another important skill we will tackle later. So, if you're cringing right now—I'd advise another career.

If you smile at the calling-in-the-(lefty)-specialist-out-of-the-bullpen-while-blaring-Metallica's-Enter-Sandman, then this may be a career for you.

On the double-mint twin side of positive, if prospects are asking to meet with you outside of regularly scheduled business hours, your odds for winning that piece of business just went up. **The stranger the date and time, the more likely you are to win**. We once had a call on Saturday at 2pm with a prospect. We won the business at 2x the price of our next closest competitor (and a good one at that).

It's easy to think of these as inconveniences and people exerting pressure on you, but you must always seek to understand (as my colleague Tim loves to talk about). If they are up to their eyeballs in work and asking to speak at 7 pm—take the call recognizing their tough hours. Perhaps it's not workload, perhaps they are in another time zone! Or, most important to consider, they are at a conference. Moral of the story—accept meetings at odd hours—they will do you a lot of good in life.

Action Item: Balance is vital. You don't want to say I'm wide open and being mistaken for not in demand. I recommend providing 2 to 3 time windows that vary. For instance, if it's a 30-minute meeting, offer 90-minute windows. For 60-minute meetings, offer 120–180-minute windows. If you work outside 9 to 5 hours, let them you're also available in the AM or PM and provide the time slots in case it's hard to block off after the e-mail exchange.

65. Seeks Advice/Input From Clients and Prospects (2 minutes)

As salespeople, we often become so engrained in the mindset that people naturally do not want to talk to us/our company that we lose sight of what our companies have to offer our clients.

As Jerry Acuff writes in his book *The Relationship Edge*, there are 13 fundamental things about human beings, and two of them can be accomplished in one fell swoop: the need to be listened to fully and the need to feel important. How can you do this? By seeking advice and input from your clients.

There are many ways to do this, but the one way I'd focus in on, if possible, is to add them to (or if you're working at a smaller company—create) a client advisory board. These boards would be pilot/test groups for new releases of solutions, would have input in what they want to see rolled out from your company in the future via a roadmap and several other "we value your opinion" types of asks.

These types of asks are best for director- and VP-level contacts who are focused on building their brand and adding line items to their resumes for that next-level job. By enabling your clients to grow their careers by gaining valuable skills or credentials your company has to offer, you're showcasing you're more than a sales person, you're a "process improvement specialist," as Jill Konrath remarks in her book *Snap Selling*. On top of being a process improvement specialist, for this client example, you're a personal brand builder.

This is not only beneficial to your clients but also to you as it is a great way to see where you can improve. Perhaps your time to deliver the work wasn't preventing this client from purchasing, but they can point out how much longer your delivery/rollout is than your competitors or how it's been hurting your reputation among their professional network.

This skill also ties in closely to (preview coming!) skill #57; building a sense of belonging to a common objective. How? Because you're getting your client involved and are both working toward a mutual goal. They have some skin in the game and **want to see you succeed because it will correlate to their own rise in importance.**

Action Item: Arrange for an executive introduction from your company to their senior level (1 to 2 below C-suite) to discuss what they'd like to see by joining your company's client advisory board.

64. Is Disciplined (Avoids Selling too Early) (2 minutes)

If I had a time machine to go back and fix (this and trying to fit a square peg in a round hole) my mistakes from the beginning of my sales career, this is the one that tops the list. We as salespeople work so hard to find a good fit that when someone is genuinely interested and recognizes our strengths, we jump through the roof and begin talking all about our great solutions! FINALLY! Finally someone who gets it! I never thought I'd finally see the day!

Michael Bosworth captures this feeling well and warns against its byproduct when he says, "The excitement of a perfect match can cause sellers to **prematurely elaborate**. The more excitement for the solution, the less they listen."[1]

Wait, wait, wait. They bought into the idea, AND get it—shouldn't you show your passion and knowledge by talking about your products? The answer? No. Because whether or not the potential customer knows it, this is a test. They are baiting you into the trap of: this person is just trying to sell me something. Think about it, ever walk into your favorite store and commend their work before looking around? If the associate started pushing things on you, did you pull back? Of course you did! Why? Because no one, ever, likes to be sold. People are predisposed to distrust you, so don't blow it the moment they start buying in.

The fact of the matter is you can never really get excitable about a deal to a client. Act like you've been there and make it routine. To use another analogy, if you've ever had a rocky flight and the pilot landed it masterfully, when you see them at the end of the flight, don't they look calm and collected? Of course they do. Why? Because that feeling of safety and security is what you're buying. You don't want some excitable "Oh my god we landed" kind of pilot. You want, No Big Deal. And that's what you are- No Big Deal. Even for the Big Deals.

Action Item: Think of Mike Weinberg's handy comparison about flight: there's a time to take off, a time to cruise at altitude, and a time to land.[2] Don't try to land when you are cruising. After the deal is done, show your gratitude through personalized notes and gifts (in accordance with federal laws of course).

63. Listens and Connects Similarities, Notes Differences (2 minutes)

Connecting similarities and noting differences is one of the easiest and best ways to frame a discussion. It enables you to implement so many successful strategies for sales. How?

Well first, it accomplishes what every potential buyer views as the very first check box in a successful sales relationship—being heard. Discussing similarities opens the floor to offering, and more than likely, sharing, stories. Telling stories (as we will discuss later) also gets your client to relax and be more receptive to your dialogue moving forward.

Now many folks are good at connecting similarities and have some baseline abilities to share stories. Where people aren't quite as comfortable—not by a longshot—is noting differences.

Noting differences in addition to sharing your similarities ensures the client was heard correctly and your desire to close, win, or otherwise act in your own selfish interest didn't clout your hearing, judgment or processing ability to move forward in the best direction for them. However notating differences is not only uncomfortable, it's difficult, and anything difficult requires practice to master.

Deb Calvert in her book *Discover Questions* offers the advice to focus your listening on what is unfamiliar because it will prevent you from trying to "one-up" your client's last sentence and/or interrupting their next sentence. In this way, **noting differences is directly tied to an improvement in active listening;** a top 10 skill.

If you're successful on both sides of the makeshift Venn diagram, when you speak next, your words won't be muddled by neither concealed disapproval nor prejudgment on the part of your prospect. Instead, they will want to hear your now "expert opinion." What may have been viewed as an interruption is now an invitation. Even if nothing else changed, you're suddenly speaking in a way that helps them, and your explanations might be able to help them with this (now more pressing) need.

Action Item: Read David Maister's *The Trusted Advisor* and his 11 steps to relationship-building. Hint: Listening for differences is one of the 11 ☺.

62. Introduces Solutions in A Scaled-Down Approach (2 minutes)

Back to relativity. As we began discussing the concept earlier in the book, we brought up lauded author Robert Cialdini and his book *Influence*. Relativity does not only apply to the gradual improvements people often make but also to your engagements and offers. If you start by positioning something that is say, $50,000 and they say no—you'll have a much more difficult time asking for them to invest $200,000 on your next go-round, no matter how great a potential fit it is.

Cialdini goes into detail about this with how sometimes people will ask for a lot of your time but then position their next ask as a far smaller ask; if you can't give 10 hours/week, can you just help with this one two-hour event?

Lesson learned is to **ask for your big fish first**, so the next fish is a willing compromise.

While settling for the smaller fish under the land and expand premise is often a strong idea to build the foundation to a strong relationship, it is important to consider the circumstances. If it's the middle of a large transformation, don't be pitching a single project, as someone else could be in there taking the lion's share. Or worse, you find out they were going throw a massive change and they gave this one project to their transformation vendor/partner to gain economies of scale/eliminate vendor setup.

On the flip side of the coin, if Newton's law of inertia is in effect, look for ways you can begin a mutually beneficial relationship. This latter circumstance is how most companies get familiar with a new vendor. Think of it as getting into a pool, most people go in gradually, they don't dive right in. They like to get acclimated to the water. *Getting acquainted by getting acclimated.*

Action Item: For inert prospects, think, *how can they dip their toe in the water?* What's the best way for them to get acquainted with our company? Where will we have the greatest opportunity to "land and expand" our business? For all other prospects, think, what's the biggest need for them, and where are we delivering differentiated, high/quick ROIs to clients?

61. Two Ears, One Mouth Advocate (2 minutes)

A lot of times we go into a meeting, prepared. We know all of our solutions, we studied their company thoroughly, know a lot about them, and are ready to… *vomit*.

I don't mean you're nervous (even though you very well could be), but I mean the verbal vomit; the relentless recitation of all you know and how impressed they should be. As a byproduct of our entrancement with ourselves, we talk. A lot. Leaving the meeting, we pat ourselves on the back—I got through this, and that, that too and oh yeah, we even covered that.

What you may not realize is that you taught a lot, but **you were meant to be the student**, learning about them. As such, you should focus your time on listening and learning.

Two ears, one mouth is an old adage, but one that is still worthwhile today. I know there are many experts out there, some of which claim the ideal ratio is 80/20—to listen 80 percent of the time and speak 20. While a commendable goal, I think the practical application of that is limited as people do want to assess a fit and "size you up" at the same time you're learning about them. Therefore, I personally like the 66 percent listening, 34 percent speaking allocation that the time-tested phrase proportions us.

Action Item: Practice makes perfect. Prepare in advance, and do some trial runs of how you think the conversation will ACTUALLY go. None of this faking it stuff that sales managers and colleagues do to make you feel better. If you expect reticence—test it out. If you expect starting or staying off course, test it. Have someone log how long you're speaking. See what the results turn out to be.

If you're struggling, come up with some valuable "Vision" questions like Walk me through, Describe to me, and so on. For more vision questions, take a look at *Questions That Sell* by Paul Cherry.

CHAPTER 5

60 to 51: Becoming an Ally

60. Diligently (Pre) Addresses Problem-Solving (2 minutes)

The worst thing in a potential pursuit is to know something is going to be an issue and to try the pray it away approach; the... "I really hope this doesn't come up." As my old director used to say, *Hope is not a strategy.*

If you know something is going to be an issue, what are you going to do to prepare for it? How will you coordinate/choreograph your responses? The biggest part about solving problems/resolving objections is it's not a monologue and it's certainly not a one-step move; it's chess, not checkers.

Before any finalist meeting, you should ask yourself what problems do we not want to come up? And then focus time on those very items to make sure you have it covered. If you address the worst thing that can happen before it happens, guess what? **It's no longer the worst thing that can happen**—you can save those concerns for tripping on your way into the meeting.

Solving problems is one of the biggest ways to showcase your value as a sales person because, frankly, most people think you're just some talkative, persuasive, self-concerned person, and until you show them otherwise—the mindset will continue. If you can show your team that you can see around corners, they will begin to listen to you and watch you with a certain amount of awe. If you can resolve top client concerns with detail and ease; you just took a giant load off their back.

About two years ago I went into a meeting knowing what their major concern would be the fact they were an unhappy client six years ago and left us. An uphill challenge for sure but one I wanted a concerted, coordinated response on prepared in advance. Our team's reply was flawless; four points delivered by three people with measurable KPIs and resolutions.

Unfortunately, for us, the CFO was a no show in the meeting—his mind was already made up regardless of what we shared. Still, I'm proud of the way we prepared to handle this question because it was infinitely more important (much to our dismay) than anything we'd be sharing about our tools and savings levers.

Action Item: What are you desperately hoping won't come up in the meeting? Rank those top 3 concerns in order of severity and triage appropriately.

Which ones are best to address before they even ask? Which ones should you not bring to light? For those, how will you respond, and who will do the talking? What are their credentials on the response subject matter?

59. Reduces Client Workload (2 minutes)

People outside of sales often ask me what the keys are to selling or where I begin with a client. While many of the answers I won't spoil (as they are most often found in the top 10 skills section), one is I start with the mindset of "How can I make this person/company's life easier?"

By starting here, I'm able to approach from a new perspective; theirs, not mine. When I'm reaching out about partnerships, introducing them to potential clients for them, our company as a buyer of their services, and so on, I'm opening their mind up to viewing our relationship as strategic. **Not sales-oriented but better business-oriented.** When you shift your perspective, theirs will follow.

A funny thing happens when you start this better business approach; these prospective clients want to know more about what you have to offer from your own bag of tools.

If this guy is this focused on driving better business results for us in areas tangential to his core focus, what can he do for us within the world he operates in everyday?

And voila, they are now seeking you out.

An important distinction here is this cannot be something that has a price tag attached. If it does, drop the price tag and make the investment in this potential relationship upfront. If you and your manager don't have the authority to do that, look into making fees contingent upon success or potential rebates (money upfront but credited back for hiring your company, etc.). While contingencies are valid to use, I'd really advocate dropping the price tag altogether, save your contingencies for the "put your money where your mouth is" part of the negotiation.

One client we were pursuing came to us with a request for funds toward a charitable cause and sponsorship of an event. Getting money for items like this is pulling teeth in large companies, so what we offered instead was something they needed: peer group benchmarking data (de-identified of course) at no cost.

I notified them that we were unable to give physical dollars but did want to contribute something at no cost to help them open up their budgets internally to fund this important event. Was it exactly what they wanted? Of course not. Did it help us make their lives easier in more than one way? Absolutely. That now client has been one of our most successful to this day.

Action Item: How can you make their life easier? Is it benchmarking information? Trend data? Helpful third- party reports to validate a process, system or procedure? Guide of some sort? Introduction of something/someone else? A sample RFP as they begin the process? Think of what you can add that is uniquely valuable in making their life easier.

58. Knows and Avoids Salesy Trigger Words (2 minutes)

"Haven't I seen this 'once in a lifetime'
business opportunity before?"

Figure 5.2 *Once in a lifetime!*

In my introduction, I talk about the "make one false move and you're dead" mentality people carry with them while meeting salespeople. They are reticent to trust you and often know they need to be open to hearing about new ideas but typically aren't ready. They are either trying to reassure themselves they are already well-covered or looking to find a reason not to like you. Think of Jason Alexander in *Shallow Hal* and the Big Toe. Something so minor gets blown out of proportion, so they will not work with you.

There's no easier way to be written off than to utilize a salesy trigger word. What are they? Let's get them on the table to ensure you don't use them at the table. Without further ado, here's the table:

Suspect	Cringe-worthy	Never-see-them again
Leader	Trust me	I'll be honest with you
Best	What do I need to do…	Buddy, pal, sport, champ
Unique	Deal	Have I got a deal for you
Very, way (adverb)	Mr. (title here)	Once-in-a-lifetime opportunity
Wouldn't you agree	What's it going to take	Do me a favor
Cheap	Don't you want to	
Feature	Pitch	
I wanted, I'd love to	Prospect	
Obviously	Just checking in	
Objection	Commission/quota/internal sales target related words	
Cutting-edge/innovative	*Last word preceding a question mark, emphasized*	
Just (any time period longer than 10 minutes)	Close (in relation to signing an agreement)	

I've put these in three different categories because, fortunately, some are just overused, meaningless words that run amuck in the sales world and clue people back into the fact you're in sales, while others are showstoppers. Don't believe me?

I once had a meeting with a CFO, and after a 45-minute meeting, he agreed to a second meeting. Pretty normal until he added in the reason why he accepted. He said that I have one phrase I hate to hear, and if I do hear it, I won't invite that person back—"I'll be honest with you." We all chimed in saying, well of course, it calls into question what you were doing with every word before that and every word after that isn't prefaced in the same way. Sounds simple but it's **one of those knee-jerk, reflexives** that some of us wouldn't even notice came out of our mouth. After all, it's an expression for a reason: people use it.

No need to beat this one to death—study the preceding table. E-mail me with questions.

Action Item: Add to my preceding table! Write down the words you roll your eyes at—your clients are probably doing the same. Do a control-find (and replace) before sending out that RFP or important e-mail. Check out Lee Salz's list for another take on the words that make people cringe.

57. Builds a Sense of Belonging and Commitment to an Objective (2 minutes)

In my first 6 months at Mercer, I was called onto a project as an SME. A massive telecom company was looking into Oracle as well as other technologies, and having come from Oracle for 4.5 years, I was called on as an expert. I learned a lot over my two days among a project team of 40 (larger than some employers I've worked with), but nothing stood out quite like drinks after the project kickoff.

One guy, we will call him Ted, was so strangely proud of the project name and logo he came up with. This is HR technology, Ted, let's not get too carried away I thought to myself. But as I look back on what is one of our 20 largest (out of 12,000) U.S. clients, I see the skill the client manager and team were able to instill. This gentleman felt:

1. A sense of belonging to something big
   and
2. A commitment to transformational change

He was a pivotal part of the project. He knew he had several resume line items out of this one effort. He knew he was climbing while building something big. He had a voice. And, he thanked *US* for it! Hard to picture clients being borderline obsequious to you, but it can happen.

As Sinek would tell you in his *Start With Why*, it's because Ted was **inspired, not manipulated**. He was "building a cathedral," as opposed to cementing some rocks together. He felt like he was a part of something big, and his name would be on this project as an example of transformational innovation for decades to come.

It's easy to point out why this is important (greater camaraderie, higher likelihood of buying, adhering to a timeline, overcoming obstacles, etc.), but it's hard to envision exactly how to build a sense of belonging. Therefore, we can shift over early to some action items:

Action Item: Think of a project name, logo, result impact (resume, promotion, raise) that will motivate your clients to reach higher or go further.

56. Effectively Confirms a Mutually Agreeable Agenda (2 minutes)

So many of us are so excited to get a meeting that we don't want to do anything to jeopardize it from happening. Why send an agenda when it can get shut down and then I miss my monthly meeting goals? I'll tell you why.

Author Mike Weinberg summarizes the need for a confirmed agenda best when he correlates setting an agenda with (you, the sales professional) running and controlling the meeting. When you don't have an agenda in place, it's not that there is no agenda, it's that *you're on the client's agenda*. The problem with that is when you're on the client's agenda, you can forget about accomplishing your asks or probing for pain.

For any of my Will Ferrell fans reading, I like to think of *Step Brothers* and their interview scene—we're conducting this interview now, not you! A funny comparison but one that is both memorable and meritorious. If you don't have an agreed-upon agenda, **you allow the client to turn the table** and put you on the defensive.

Now, for many of my relationship-oriented sellers, I understand not every meeting is going to have a step-by-step agenda, and it shouldn't. However, you should have an understanding of the topics that will be discussed or their items of interest before you schedule an in-person meeting. If you don't and still want to meet, consider running a networking event; something informal that allows you to say hello and get to know them while maximizing your time by saying hello to other prospects and/ or setting up introductions for them to meet clients.

If you're not bought into the idea of getting a confirmed agenda in advance, let me imbue some additional wisdom. Setting an agenda differentiates you from other sales folks, and while it may seem elementary or corny at first glance, your client will appreciate how prepared you are. After all, you took the time in advance to look out for their calendar ("just imagine what they will do for me as a client" is running through their mind).

Last but not least, setting an agenda helps prevent the perennial push (in perpetuity). Accepting a meeting is easy when you can ignore it. Without an agenda, you're just some guy (or gal) looking to schmooze me, and while I'm open to the idea of being schmoozed and a new potential busi-ness partner, it's not a big focus of mine. So, I'll push. And push again. Suddenly, I'm not sure why I accepted the meeting in the first place. Today's world is a short-attention, short-term-memory one, so give them the easy ability to recall your importance.

Action Item: Read Mike Weinberg's *New Sales. Simplified* and his section on sharing the agenda; first get buy-in and then seek input.

55. Captivates Audience Through Candidacy and Humor (3 minutes)

In my readings, I came across one particularly poignant (say that five times fast) section from *Ted Talks* around the dual battle we face when presenting; the ability to capture someone's attention in the first 10 seconds and then compel them forward (sometimes quite literally onto the edge of their seat) in the next 60.

Put another way, what's your hook? And then, what's your transition? So often, in business, we go into meetings without even giving someone a shot. I do it. You do it. We all do it. While this isn't a Charmin ultra-soft commercial, it's an important reality. So. how are you turning the tide?

The two ways I see people do it effectively are (1) candidacy and (2) (you guessed it!) humor. By candidacy, I mean calling things out for the boring way they usually are or the status quo and how you're different. Different engages (provided that you actually deliver). Candid, blunt, frank—these words create interest. See how you can use them to self-deprecate in a way that **creates interest and showcases your difference**.

One example that comes to mind is taking advantage of how in the HRIS space, experts (Gartner) say core competencies between SAP, Oracle and Workday are less than 0.3 (on a scale of 5) apart. Call this out and discuss how the evaluation is about what specialty areas are important to you, who you feel best supported by, confident in a successful rollout, assured of long-term partnership, and so on.

The second is the more common route—humor.

Now I'm sure many of you are conjuring images of jokes that don't land or terrible office attempts at humor about playing golf or the weather. Humor doesn't have to be difficult, even if you aren't funny. Trust me, I'm sure you realized I'm not a standup comic, but even I have landed a jab or two. Allow me to share.

One of the best ways to joke is to poke fun at yourself and/or your own stock imagery in a presentation. I once saw a vendor rally a sales organization after a full day of windowless presentations by joking about how his stick figure didn't even have eyebrows—"geez, I mean I know I'm not much to look at, but come on marketing—can't you at least give me eyebrows!"

I was able to bridge a sensitive group (15 person finalist meeting) by having a title slide with an image of a gentleman writing equations on a glass wall and saying: we WILL discuss Benefits stewardship and brokerage, I'm NOT sure we will get a chance to color on the glass, might not have enough time. People jumped in with their own jokes and a certain kind of vibrancy and reality was brought into the conversation to lighten the mood and keep people intrigued by what I would say next.

Action Item: Ask someone to keep you on a timer. Did you hit your opening? Was there something in your next 60 seconds that built off your candidacy? Or, was there a good transition from your humor?

54. Shifts Conversation From Products
to Solutions (2 minutes)

One of the biggest ways to distinguish yourself as providing a solution as opposed to pitching a product is to shift the focus of your outreach from "why you're so great" to "why you, Prospect X, should be focused on this issue because of its impact of X KPI or Y MTM" (metrics that matter from Jeb Blount's *Inked*).

I work for a company that delivers considerable value specifically because of its size. As the largest broker, we have the most clout. There are many numbers to back this up, but many times, the numbers, even when accepted as correct, do not resonate. People have skepticism because you are showing them why you are great—which has a direct correlation to your pocket. When discussing how they were struggling to save money and how their premiums/costs continued to rise, I shifted the focus from why we are the best choice given our #1 position, to the benefits they would see with a Tier 1 (three organizations) broker.

This catches people off-guard and therefore gets them to drop their guard a bit. What did he say? He's recommending more than just himself? Prospects then interrupt with considerable dialogue on who do I consider a Tier 1 broker, how specifically these three companies make a difference and then, the best softball question I could get, well then how do you differentiate yourself from the other 2?

Just remember an important old adage, *if you say it, it's sold, but if they say it, it's gold.* In this case, the prospect is not only engaging (meaning their retention of the information goes up dramatically), but they are helping build the case for change AND for your company!

I know this is a rather specific example, but to provide a framework, think of what problem you are solving (rising costs, business complexity, risk, retention), what benefit they will see (reduced time to hire, risk mitigation, reduced costs, automation), and who can significantly help them (2 to 3 industry players, one of which is yours I'd hope). On this last section, for those really sitting pretty in their pipeline, don't feel obligated to include your company!

If you're not best suited for that piece of business, let them know. One of the perennial top producers at my company says he recommends our solutions 80 percent of the time. 80 percent may sound like you're fore-going 20 percent more revenue, but it's actually a fantastic way to keep 20 percent of your population open to listening to you for years to come. What's the price you'd pay for that?

Action Item: Get buy-in to the solution area before buy-in on your company; it harbors good sentiments and showcases you're looking out for them versus your bank account.

53. Builds Credibility (2 minutes)

One of the most important attributes out there for sales professionals is credibility. And yet, I see very few people taking active steps to build it! I can see some of you thinking, "Alex if it's so important, why is it ranked 53rd?" Fair point. I have this one lower on the list because while it is extremely important, it is extremely hard to do quickly and is perhaps the biggest commitment of any of the skills.

Credible and trusted are probably the two words I see used most casually in sales. I think this is a systemic societal issue that people over-use these words, but it's also because there is a **continuum**. If the words credible and trusted were on a 1 to 10 scale, where would you feel comfortable calling yourself credible or trusted? Well I'm sure for many of you, it's at 5 (average score), or for others, it's at 7 (passing score in school), but yet so many celebrate when they get to stage 1! Look Ma, I made it!

This is something we all suffer from because it takes so long to even make it to Step 1, and once we get there, we think it's good enough. Why? Because it's better than 95 percent of others out there. But, to truly stand out and make yourself an inbound recipient, as opposed to a respected outbound caller, you'll need to build your personal value statement.

To enhance your credibility, consider taking actions in several of the following eight areas:

- Personal website: Can you build a transparent, nonself-serving site that showcases value for your buyers? Not you, not your company, it's about your buyers and/or your industry.
- Groups: What groups can you join to be a consistent face and voice? Think of industry groups, peer groups, membership bodies focused on similar roles, alumni groups, and so on.
- Partnerships: Who can you help that will feel obligated to help you? A correlated solution? Someone else serving a similar role to your clients? Someone else serving your clients?

- Networking, conferences: What groups can you join in the background as a participant to gain credibility as a curious learner, as opposed to a desperate seller?
- Speaking opportunities: On the flip side, where can you speak to a group about something that resonates with, or enlightens, them?
- White papers/research reports: What can you write or share that will resonate?
- Newspaper article or comments: Where can you establish a consistent, bi-directional dialogue with potential prospects and/or partners?
- LinkedIn articles: What can you write about that has a common, unique theme and differentiates your voice?

Action Item: Focus in on two of the preceding bullets and get started!

52. Offers Clients a Conceptual Future State (2 minutes)

As many adroit salespeople know, opening is one of the most important parts of your job. The demo, the consultants' credentials; it's your job to bolster them and start off on the right foot. In fact, it's been researched and proven. Neil Rackham in his book *Spin Selling* shows the vital importance of the first two minutes of any conversation—that's when clients and prospects determine how tuned in they will be for your discussion/demonstration.

While many are aware of these facts and skilled at delivering them, they (including myself) miss a key part of the process that is usually right at the ¾ mark. Step four on David Maister's five-step trust building process in *The Trusted Advisor*: envision.

When clients embark upon an evaluation journey, the road may seem long and arduous; enough for them to pull away after thinking of the first two, three, maybe four, steps. They may never **visualize the actual finish line.**

This is where you need to step in to help. Offering up this visualization of success will help them buy into the project (as outlined in skill #57) and further believe in its potential success. Speaking of success; put outcomes in the context of your prospect's personal and professional success. After all, *people win* not companies.

The beauty of successfully framing a conversation and introducing a conceptual future state is that it not only creates a goal for them to grasp, it creates a dialogue. Now clients are not only buying into the future state you have proposed, they have the opportunity to have a voice in the process and begin to mold that idea into their own. Suddenly, they are moving past the ideation stage and mapping out the entire project roadmap. The questions you'd normally ask, they are asking for your input or confirmation.

Sometimes, to paint a beautiful picture, you just need to set the canvas next to the beach and let someone else do the work.

Action Item: Work on your segue questions to get into painting this picture/envisioning the successful future state. Phrases like "Picture this," "Imagine," "Wouldn't it be great if," "Just think in" can do you a lot of good to get their *creativity* to inspire *mobility*.

51. Minimizes Asks (2 minutes)

Perhaps the most oppositional or controversial section you'll find in my book is this section right here. Why? Because it's counterintuitive.

For my entire sales career, I've heard about how you need to ask for the meeting and you need to ask for the sale, yet I haven't seen much to prove that value, especially, and emphatically, when it comes to prospecting.

People know what your end goal is because frankly—it's the same as just about everyone else's. You're looking to do business with them or get more business from them/their clientele.

The structure to my prospecting e-mails looked pretty much the same for years: a personalized intro showcasing I did my homework, an area to explore potential value/fit, and a close asking for a time and date to speak. Look familiar? We've all had pretty similar training.

What I've noticed is that asking for the meeting is in almost direct opposition (in the prospect's perception) to sincerely employing give to get (a top 10 skill). Why? Because it's a reminder that you are looking for something from them, so all the value you had offered up gets negated as you bring them back down to reality with the focus ending on you and your needs.

Now some of you will argue that people will take advantage, or that without the ask, you'll make zero progress. However, as Jerry Acuff says in his book *The Relationship Edge*, "When you provide real value to people, they want to reciprocate."[1] Therefore you should **focus less on your follow-up tactics and more on the level of value you are providing**. As I've mentioned in the past, there are many skilled outbound sellers, but few (self-generated) inbound recipients.

Action Item: Leave off the closing "meeting request" on your first 2 to 3 outreaches. This will help you lay the groundwork for providing value and avoid the misperception that you're self-serving. Track your client responsiveness as compared to the e-mails you included a call to action for a meeting.

If it's markedly higher, continue on. If it isn't, your request for a meeting after delivering three valuable messages will be received much better nonetheless.

CHAPTER 6

50 to 41: Developing a Potential Partnership Together

50. Anticipates Needs (2 minutes)

Growing up, in my teenage years, one of my favorite movies was *Enemy of the State*. It was a movie about one man overcoming serious obstacles from a seemingly unbeatable organization.

Why were they unbeatable? Because not only did they have so much power, but they were so well prepared. Jack Black, as one of the operational assets, was famous for always suavely saying "It's already done." It's a phrase that has stuck with me for years (just like "Execute!" in *Captain Phillips*) as it was the pinnacle mark of preparation. Oftentimes I ask myself, "how am I preparing myself in advance to provide the cock-sure "It's already done" to my manager or client?" It's a statement that speaks volumes; not only did you have the foresight to know it was important, you did it ahead of time, without anyone asking and in the best interest and benefit of someone else. So, what have you (already) done?

Let me provide some good examples of getting out ahead of things.

In my world of benefits brokerage, most clients have plans starting on the 1/1 calendar year with Open Enrollment taking place in November. As opposed to me waiting to see how Open Enrollment went, I can get out ahead of the communication by sending them an Open Enrollment checklist/guide in late September to help them prepare properly/check that they did everything right. Step 2? I can send them tips on managing the Open Enrollment process at the end of October.

While this is a specific example, the premise holds true across many roles and industries. If someone asks for something around a certain time each year/quarter, don't wait for the ask—show you are paying attention and give it to them a week before they'd ask.

This does not have to apply solely to client and prospect delivery enablement/work, you can apply the anticipating needs skill to any pursuit. For example, they are likely going to have to build a case to finance or their executive team to get approval, so give them a case study, ROI example, and synopsis of key facts in a framework they can take to their internal team. If their competitors or the industry as a whole are doing something almost universally, note it to them and showcase how they can implement it.

There are many ways to anticipate needs, and in a world where most are reacting to change: showcase your ability to anticipate.

Action Item: Sync this skill with your calendaring skill. What things come up every year for that role, industry, client? When is the proper advanced notice to send them help? Will they appreciate it? How much frontend work does it require? Do a cost–benefit analysis to see where you can make the biggest impact at the smallest frontend time requirement and focus on what is scalable.

49. Doesn't Push an Agenda (2 minutes)

People often ask me how I like Mercer, why I chose Mercer, and if I like Mercer better than Oracle. They are not surprised when I tell them I like Mercer more, but for reasons different than their perception that Oracle is cut-throat and treats you like a number as opposed to a person. Firstly—I didn't have that experience at Oracle. Second—the number one most common reply I provide is I love Mercer because I don't have to push an agenda.

I'm fortunate at Mercer to have an expansive toolchest that allows me to be a jack of all trades when it comes to getting your HR house in order. While many may view the number of offerings as a lot of clutter and a lot of trouble to go through to learn, I'd suggest finding a company that lets you diversify for a number of reasons.

For personal growth, you can develop more skill sets and meet with more people. Hence, you're constantly learning and evolving. Second, however, is this point that you don't have to push, segue, harken back to, or any other phrase meaning discuss your agenda. When you don't have your agenda to focus on in an introductory meeting, **you can really focus on what the client wants, and you can actively listen.** When you have one area you can help in, you're making disjointed, forced attempts to steer the conversation back to your product line—a losing recipe for building rapport and earning trust. If you're not pushing an agenda, you're less likely to be waiting to speak, which is what most people in a conversation do.

Now for those who think they caught me in an inconsistent web, let me make the distinction between setting and pushing an agenda. Setting an agenda shows you're prepared, consider their time valuable, and provide insight into the flow of the meeting (usually for meeting #2 and beyond). Pushing an agenda shows you're self-serving and looking for how the client can help you, as opposed to how you can help them.

Action Item: For your first meetings, go in with an open notebook and pencil. Mike Weinberg talks more about this *in New Sales. Simplified.* But, I must say I agree. Have some materials in your back pocket, should the client be looking for supporting information, but it's imperative not to lead with this.

A blank slate, while it may look unprepared, is the best way to approach an introduction. A doctor doesn't come in with presentations on his highest margin treatments or guesses what's wrong with you, he starts with you talking and him listening. Listening to see where his expertise may help solve your pains (little more literal than us).

48. Motivates Others to Act (2 minutes)

Sales personnel have to be leaders. Why? Because others are staid in their old ways. Status quo, inertia—these are byproducts of comfort. You're most likely going to have to get others to act through inspiration and incentivization.

One way I've found helpful is to point out the rewards that can come for them personally. Things like career progression, a high-profile client, a new peer to their existing client book of business, and so on do a lot to remind people of the value you can bring to not only the company, but the value you can bring to them.

The key here is to not oversell it. No one likes to feel like they're being sold on an idea—not your clients and not your colleagues or partners. Also, if people are going to do your bidding for you, make sure it's legitimate. No one wants to expedite or escalate unless it's absolutely necessary because if it turns out to not be just a passing interest, their image, alongside yours, wains, and after 2 to 3 more, they are the boy who cried wolf.

One of the best pieces of advice I can give is to make yourself easy to help. You'll be asking for lots of help from many different groups of people, so make sure you set appropriate standards in advance and use the tools at your disposal to do the lion's share of the work for them. Think of them as clients signing a contract; they should have just a few line items needing their attention, and they can fill in the blanks, as opposed to creating something from scratch. If you're pioneering a new idea, do it yourself and let them adapt off of your example. Their creative and hardworking juices may start flowing, so they create something entirely different, and if they don't, at least they are modifying your template to help spread the word and give you more backing.

As it pertains to timing, be courteous. If something isn't urgent, note it. If it is, do that too. Don't use the urgent note (in subject line or Outlook flag) on your first outreach (pending an emergency).

When it comes to motivating people, **incentivization and isolation** (asking for specific, minor details) are often quite helpful tactics. Inspiration, your third pillar in motivation, is far more difficult and has the risk of coming across as disingenuous, so I'd be careful employing this pillar too often.

Action Item: What are some ways you can do a better job to isolate your ask? Go through your asks from the colleague's point of view; how long did it take to read your e-mail? To do the work? To send a reply? Do these things yourself to get an honest appreciation of their time—it'll help you minimize your asks going forward.

47. Checks in With the Client on Meeting Direction (2 minutes)

Oftentimes, sales people look for something to say in the meeting. Assuming it's not self-promotion, I get it. It's a change of pace, it's a **needed interruption to the monotonous** drudging on. Your easiest ways to take a quick break in the action are:

1. To see if things are clear
2. Resonant with your client/that client's team
3. You're hitting on their key points

An effective agenda is a big step in this battle, but it's not the final straw. Take, for example, the world I live in—brokerage. There is a big difference between savings and cost reductions, and that might not be perfectly articulated. Your client could think your definition of savings is about reduction in commissions and fees, whereas you're going on about cost savings from other improvements. While still valuable, they may want to hear more about your fee reductions versus their incumbent, service-level guarantees (SLAs), Performance Guarantees (PGs), and so on. Checking in with the client to make sure you're hitting the mark is a perfect invitation to let them put their hand up.

Many of you may be thinking, my clients are more than willing to jump in and correct us or tell us when we are missing the mark. While that may be true, there comes a point where they may stop jumping in. It's either fear of "we don't speak the same language" or ammunition against you for the cynic sitting quietly ready to pounce when you leave the room and for he/she to say: See, they don't get it, they were way off base talking about X when we wanted to discuss Y.

If people aren't asking questions, it's one of two reasons—they already have their mind made up or they aren't interested (now). If their mind is made up, this much needed break in the action will highlight that: good or bad. Same goes for if they are not interested.

The last point I will make is: this is a way to ensure you let the client know they have a voice and they are being heard; you are putting their priorities ahead of your own.

Action Item: Develop an agenda slide that is hyperlinked to each section. If clients want to start on Section 5, click the link and jump down. It's a subtle change but it shows you considered their intentions and planned to accommodate in advance.

46. Asks Effective Questions (2 minutes)

There isn't a single sales guru out there who wouldn't advocate the importance of asking effective questions. Books and books are dedicated to the topic, and others have large sections about their importance. So my question is, if this is so widely proclaimed as mission critical by every expert, how are the majority of sales organizations doing nothing to build questioning skillsets or build effective question playbooks?

If there is any advice I'd give to readers, it's to **read sales books for the questions they pose in each situation and adapt/adopt them for your own use.** No sense in completely reinventing the wheel when for 90 percent of your competitors, they haven't even considered the fact that there is a wheel at all.

Effective questions have a few things in common. They are *Thought-Provoking, *Client-Centric, and *Value-Oriented. As this is easier to say than do, let's take a look at a sampling baker's dozen of my favorite effective questions:

- We appreciate you reaching out/including us, what or who drew you to us?
- Who are your top three trusted advisors and how did they become such? (Jeffrey Gitomer: *Little Red Book of Selling*)
- What will make this project a success for you? Professionally? Personally?
- What do you need from me/us to ensure you and your team are successful?
- What hurdles or challenges do you expect to take place during this evaluation and how can we help tackle them?
- Would it help to see some of the sample RFPs (intros, samples, etc.) we've helped clients put together?
- What are the drawbacks for making a change? What happens if you don't change? What are the consequences?
- In the next three years, what do you think your greatest opportunity will be?

- Why do your clients buy from you? Why do your employees work here?
- What's the risk of this solution? What's the reward?
- Why now? Why is the current situation no longer tenable?
- How would you prioritize your top five criteria for making a decision? Top five metrics for success?
- Does that answer your question completely/in full?

Action Item: Track how many questions you get to ask in a typical introductory, discovery, demo, finalist, negotiation meeting. Plan a word bank of 1.5x that number to give you flexibility in the meeting while keeping a streamlined focus on providing (or rather, extracting) value.

45. Researches Effectively and Efficiently (2 minutes)

It's been said a million times that time is our most precious commodity, and it never seems to be something we have enough of (exception: 2020 coronavirus). As a salesperson, there are perhaps 500 (not exaggerating) different things you could be doing at any point in time throughout your career. Needless to say, prioritization of tasks is crucial, and working efficiently is paramount.

One of the tasks I myself and many others are guilty of is not researching effectively and efficiently. For those who know me, you're probably saying to yourself—Alex is always well versed in his client's matters and prepared—of course he researches effectively. Here comes the quantity versus quality discrepancy. While many of us may focus on the amount of research we do, it's really how we carry it out that's more important.

Someone like myself might bounce between LinkedIn, company website, Qualtrics reports from Discover.org, and the occasional Google Alert to meet an outreach, but I measure it by the outreach, not the research. Rinsing and repeating this flow is challenging because I'm constantly jockeying between solutions and my attention span is fractured. The result? A lower barometer of success. When 20 e-mails was the thought, all of a sudden, 12 is the goal.

My advice is to dedicate a 60- to 120-minute block (less than that isn't productive and more is unrealistic) where you **tackle one source**, one database, or one platform and get what you need across that vertical or target group for that day/week. This way, it isn't one-off searches you're doing; you're building toward a common goal and satisfying a linked effort. After your research is done, look over your talking points and begin to formulate an authentic, creative and personalized message.

Action Item: Now there are thousands of sources of data that constantly require updating and reviewing, so my advice is to see which ones you are comfortable with on the go. Before a follow-up meeting, check your Google Alerts and news articles and recheck their LinkedIn profile. All of these items can be done on the go. The annual reports and buying interests should be saved for your laptop. The main distinction I'd make is anything that's foundational/strategic should be done in advance from your laptop while anything relational or simple to remember can be done from your phone.

44. Leaves Each Meeting With an Agreed-Upon Action Plan (2 minutes)

My senior year of school I was down between two quotes for my year-book and while this was the losing bid on account of it being too long, I think it's perfect for what I'm about to discuss. The passage from Abdul Kalam says:

"Thinking is progress. Non-thinking is stagnation of the individual, organisation and the country. Thinking leads to action. Knowledge without action is useless and irrelevant. **Knowledge with action, converts adversity into prosperity.**"

It's a wonderfully powerful and action-oriented passage that encapsulates the reason why action plans are so important. Many of us have done lots of leg work to get a meeting, thought of all the niceties, added values, and questions to ask, but we end up leaving without doing the most important thing—the action plan. We did plenty of thinking, and that was progress. All that thinking created a wealth of knowledge, but without the action, it fizzles out—it's wasteful, and waste is harm. Harm to your prospects' calendars and KPIs and harm to your wallet (prosperity).

Don't waste your time, or theirs; ensure the momentum is kept because without momentum, nothing moves. In physics, in energy, and most of all, in sales. There are not only too many competing priorities, but there is the even more considerable danger of the feel-good, out-clause. The, "Okay, I met with *X* expert and things aren't so bad here. They didn't suggest any mutual actions so I must be in good shape!"

Once this mindset sets in, good luck. Like Leonardo DiCaprio says in *Wolf of Wall Street* (minus a few added expletives) "It'll take the National Guard to get {me} out of here!" Without a regime change or drastic organizational shift, this mindset is like cement, so your best bet is to prevent it from being poured by having action item steps forward. Concrete ones. ☺

Action Item: Sounds simple, but take notes during the meeting and close by summarizing the action items you need to take and the items where you need something (information, approvals, data, etc.) from them. Get buy-in from your clients/prospects, don't just simply state what you heard.

43. Shows Adaptation Skills Through Mirror and Matching Ability (3 minutes)

Let me share a story with you that shows the importance of mirror and matching.

I was down in Raleigh, North Carolina, presenting to a client of ours looking to win their business for HRIS software. I had gotten to know two of the key stakeholders very well over the past year and was confident about how our relationship was developing. To further cement my dedication to the opportunity, my potential future boss was there for extra support but more so to evaluate me for an open position in the field. What did this mean? It meant All. Eyes. On. Me.

We were well-prepared and delivered a complete, client-centric, energetic presentation. My key stakeholders came over to commend us on a terrific presentation; all signs pointing toward either A—landing the client or B—landing the job right? If not both I thought!

Wrong, there was one vital flaw that stuck out and the key stakeholders delicately brushed past—they relayed along that I (someone who grew up in Connecticut and was living in Massachusetts) spoke too fast and some of the committee lost interest in my presentation shortly after starting. All the other laurels went out the window because I was written off for speaking too quickly.

As a rather confident 24-year-old, I wrote that off as their loss! "Are you kidding me? You're not going to consider us because you didn't have the gall to ask me to slow down a bit? How narrow-minded?" I thought at the time. But when looking back to assign the blame—it's on me. I didn't pick up on their patterns, their cues, their disengaged looks, and to add further fuel to the fire, I dismissed their opinions as less valuable because they neither controlled the initiative nor its purse strings. However, it was I who was (politely) dismissed.

There's an old adage of how people buy from those they like. I'd argue that you can take this a step further and say people like those similar to them. If you don't believe me, take a look at dogs and their owners—how often does the dog remind you of its owner? You may be surprised to see that even with our furry four-legged friends, we seek out similarities.

My advice is to aim to mirror people's body language and match their tone and rapidity, but, most importantly, to **have a lag**. Don't start mirroring someone immediately because then they will have the adult version of repeated mimicking mockery; you know when children retort what you just said with attitude—"Are you mocking me?"

Make your mental notes to do certain things but don't force it. It's better to miss a couple opportunities to mirror or match than to force even just two. I say two because there is the benefit of the doubt you will get on the first one from an interested buyer who likes you.

Action Item: Read Daniel Pink's *To Sell is Human* and his words on strategic mimicry: watch (legs crossed, lean back, tilt, speech), wait, wane (mirror first, let go).

42. Perseveres (2 minutes)

For anyone who's seen the movie *Tommy Boy*, you realize Richard isn't a salesperson. However, he did have a couple pearls of wisdom. One of them being, "If I took no for an answer I probably would wind up on a street corner selling spicy hotdogs and wearing a funny hat." I think Richard underestimates hot dog vendors.

The point being, you can't let "No" stop you from continuing on and trying again. In my first ever sales training, the folks at Sandler had a saying, "Some Will, Some Won't; So What? Next." It's a catch-phrase that has stuck with me ever since.

There are a plethora of scary statistics out there:

× Each decision has an average of seven buyers
  Corporate Executive Board (CEB) Study
× Up to 74 percent of deals go to the first person through the door that adds value[3]
× It takes Eight attempts to reach someone, and five follow-ups when trying to earn the sale.

These statistics combined with real-world experience can make you want to give up and pick a new profession. Yours truly had that experience and thought that maybe I'd move into consulting sales, hold the sales.

The important part to remember is that despite popular opinion, everyone knows sales is difficult. If they didn't know that, they wouldn't compensate you the way they do. Don't let people tell you otherwise; deep down they know.

When it comes to particular instances of perseverance, I'm not saying to battle back after a firm "No" from a client like some intrepid stalker-movie-hero trying to overcome adversity, I'm saying to not let minor things get you down. Life itself is a struggle, and as bestselling author Mark Manson would tell you, it's about figuring out "**What pain you want to sustain?**"[1] If you like the pursuit or new business and the daily grind, keep on moving forward. Your hard work will pay off. The long hours you put in your first 2 years building out a territory? They will pay off in spades as you reap rewards in the years to follow and allow you to live a more comfortable life on a more flexible schedule.

Remember, it's a marathon, not a sprint, and in the long run, "completing a marathon makes us happier than eating a piece of chocolate cake."[2]

Action Item: No surprise here: Read Mark Manson's *The Subtle Art of Not Giving a F*ck*. See if sales is a pain you want to sustain, if you enjoy the process and not just the end result, and if it's something you want to leave as part of your legacy.

41. Negotiates to Objectives, Not Asks (3 minutes)

In sales, I notice a tendency to feel like you have to immediately solve problems. There isn't a situation truer than in sales negotiations. Sales representatives across all industries around the world tend to panic when they hear the client needs a 20 percent discount. Franticly, they take it as a verified fact and go to management to get a discount; sometimes without ever asking a single question. You've done well to ask many questions leading up to this process, why stop now?

Let's help ease the concern. First off—"get me a 10% discount" or "I just need 10% off" is not negotiating. Respectively, it's demanding and it's asking. Both of which require even more questions than negotiating as you're further away from the root of the issue. Remember that because people are so conditioned to asking for discounts, it's their default too. In the case of a potential deal, it's their interpretation of what's needed to get a deal done; sometimes, it's accurate; other times, it's not the only way to look at something. Therefore, you need to see what they are looking at in order to see if your interpretation aligns with theirs. Instead of focusing on the ask, **focus on what they are looking to accomplish and why**.

Little hard to visualize, so let's walk through some examples of why clients were asking for discounts:

Funds tight in Year 1: On-ramp the key departments in Year 1 on a smaller employer population/pilot group. Years 2 and beyond, we got the full value of the original price. This was suitable for our management team, as it also showed significant growth and didn't set an expectation of discounting.

Similar competitor at 30 percent less: After we peeled back the onion, we realized the competitor was not including a number of integrations and tandem solutions that we were. As opposed to decoupling our solution set, we knew how much these items cost at our competitor and asked the client to go back to them and ask for pricing it all-in-one. We were in fact 20 percent less than the competition when all things were considered. They signed.

Top competitors at 40 percent less: Them coming back to us with this information shows we were their preferred option. Don't underestimate that.

I flushed out why we were their top choice, and they mentioned how we had stronger savings estimates but management was concerned about the sticker differential. We went to a 15 percent price premium with a 20 percent shared savings arrangement. They signed and we overachieved our initial price tag.

Action Item: Ask yourself in advance, what are they looking to accomplish with each request/ask/demand? Flush out your playbook of suitable alternatives to discounting and then ask them the same question about what they are looking to accomplish.

Don't be so concerned about how you could have gotten them lower or missed *X*. If you trust the process and reach a spot where everyone is happy—that's positioning you better for long-term success than really raking them over the coals on this first deal.

Read Jeb Blount's 3 elements of negotiation (power position, leverage, motivation) in his new book *Inked*.

CHAPTER 7

40 to 31: Becoming Their Preferred Choice

40. Demonstrates an Unflinching Curiosity
(2 minutes)

Perhaps one of the best things college taught me is to consider everything and question anything. Perhaps it worked a little too well, as now I'm questioning college's effectiveness itself.

Now it might make me a bit more of a pain in the ass to deal with than before, as I'm always unraveling people's anger to show their misunderstanding or them not seeking to understand someone's viewpoint, but it's been valuable in sales.

In life and especially in sales, it's too easy to get bogged down with frustration, anger, resentment, and any other form of negativity. However, these are all losing recipes, and the only thing they create is unproductivity. Unless you're in News.

If you take the problems people vent about and **seek to find a better one**, you're turning negativity into positivity. The conversion process looks like this: Negativity–Curiosity–Activity–Positivity (NCAP).

A simple four-step process, but it's effective. Next time you find yourself complaining about something, think about what you can do to fix it? Is it worth fixing? If it is, use your unflinching curiosity to research, write, plan, strategize, and actualize a new way. Curiosity is the gateway to success and to a better way. In sales, it can help you develop new tools and resources to help your team, the organization, or maybe even your entire company!

Curiosity's sister, self-review, also helps you question why you individually, or as a team, aren't being successful in a pursuit. In fact, if you take a closer look at anything, you'll realize curiosity is at the heart of the skill. As a matter of fact, the action of taking a closer look itself stems from curiosity.

Action Item: Little shout out to my Commence Cofounder Tim Denman for turning me onto this life vantage point: a simple acronym called ASK. ASK stands for Assume Positive Intent, Seek to Understand, Kindness (Always be kind). These three simple sentences can change your life. Keep them in your back pocket at all times.

39. Displays Passion and Positivity for Position (2 minutes)

In Daniel Pink's *To Sell is Human*, he shared a powerful statistic that insurance agents in the top decile of optimism sold 88 percent more than those in the bottom 10 percent. This statistic was powerful proof of another famous expression, "Whether you think you can or you can't, you're right."

For anyone who thinks those who are positive and happy are trying to glad-hand their way past you, let me ask you a question:

Think about every common interaction you have had surrounding a purchase.

Maybe it's an ice cream, perhaps it's at a restaurant, hell it could even be at the gas station: *if the person helping you is genuinely happy to do their job, aren't you glad you were able to do business with them?* Feels good to support their cause right? Of course it does, we admire those who are happy, despite our decreasing ability to maintain those displays of emotion as we age. Hence, why I think we are so ecstatic when we see a dog or baby. Their unencumbered joy and nonjaded perspective make us happy. Why? Because happiness, joy, positivity, and passion are **infectious**.

I vividly remember one of the times I felt most passionate and focused in life. It was just after hearing legendary stunt pilot Sean Tucker spoke at our Oracle inaugural class of training program. Sean is a particularly gifted speaker with some of the most awe-some stories you'll ever hear. His story gets you on the edge of your seat, but it's the way he fuels the story and not how the story fuels him that drives it home. I thought: This guy has found what he loves in life, and I too want that feeling.

Under that same breath, being passionate about what you do eliminates so many difficulties. So many are self-evident, but one that might not be is that passion for your position means you're more likely to be successful because of stability. If you love your job, you're likely to continue working in that industry and perhaps even at that company. That kind of stability is valuable as people look for long-term resources they can trust in a flighty (pun-intended) world.

Action Item: Remember that *aptitude + attitude = altitude*. Your success hinges upon your belief in yourself, your outlook on your future and your attitude in the moment; don't let things you can control spiral out of control. Take this following quiz to see how happy you are in your current life:

Authentichappiness.sas.upenn.edu/default.aspx

To test your resolve, check out Angela Duckworth's Grit Test here https://angeladuckworth.com/grit-scale/

Lastly, don't forget that "Pessimists are usually right but it's the optimists who change the world" (Friedman, Thomas).

38. Shows Appreciation (3 minutes)

One of the sad realities we all have to face in life is that so many people are transactional. Transactional sales, relationships based on proximity, and as Aristotle would say, many friendships of utility. Although, out of every *negative* situation lies a *positive* opportunity and that opportunity is for you. And, it starts with showing appreciation.

Showing appreciation nowadays isn't much more than a quick thanks or perhaps a thank you e-mail. However, once that person is out of that jam, they are on to the next one (cue Jay-Z). This makes it all the easier to stand out. A good starting point for elevating your appreciation is to cc the person's manager when they help you out. For someone who is bonus-eligible and/or has someone else dictating their earnings (unlike you), this can have a strong impact. In fact many companies are implementing formal kudos systems that have **direct ties on variable compensation,** so your words could equate to dollars in their pocket.

Showing appreciation doesn't have to be directly tied, in the moment, to help you received. In fact, delaying a formal thank you can actually go a longer way. Thank you cards and holiday gifts are perfect examples to consider, and they are also a way to stay front of mind to your clients and valued network. Another appreciation item to consider is sending birthday messages and cards. With LinkedIn often telling us when someone is born, send them a card or small gift in advance to connect a little more personally.

The key to remember with anything you send is the e-mail, gift, card, and so on must be genuine. Don't phone it in with some generic message and signing your name. Copy paste doesn't work here. No CTRL-C, CTRL-V.

Showing appreciation extends beyond external influences, it should also go internal.

Can I share a story with you?

When I was staffing a new opportunity, I was met with a strong amount of resistance; it was like I was inconveniencing them to do their job. As opposed to chalking it up to someone being rude, I went a step further and asked our Office Leader how our consultants are compensated.

Much to my dismay, I found out bringing in new sales revenue was a relatively small blip on their incentive compensation. This made me reflect on not only the current situation but all prior work. These are people who are integral to our success and helping me make tens of thousands of dollars, and all they are getting is a corporate pat on the back? Not on my (now thanks to them, *Breitling*) watch!

I decided it was time to get them some Christmas gifts and treat them all to lunch at a steakhouse. One of our more tenured consultants wrote me later that evening saying that no salesperson has ever done that and how thankful she was. Not only was it the right thing to do, it helped our internal image as sales personnel at the company and has boosted our relationship.

Action Item: Remember, *pigs get fed but hogs get slaughtered*. Don't be a hog. Don't be afraid to spend some money saying thank you. You'll be more successful and fulfilled in life by sharing the spoils of your success.

This extends into your referrals, references, personality insights; anyone who helps you!

37. Disrupts the Status Quo (2 minutes)

"Implementing these changes won't be easy. We're pretty set in doing things the wrong way."

Figure 7.1 It might not be verbalized, but it's internalized to keep on doing things the same way

There's an old adage I'm sure you've all heard, "If it ain't broke, don't fix it." Unfortunately, for salespersons all over the world, the definition of the word "broke" seems to be vastly different to sales people than it does to our buyers. If it's not broke, covered in toxic chemicals, *and* setting the rest of the company on fire, it seems to be put "out of sight, out of mind" (toxic chemical covered and all).

So, one of the toughest questions to answer is, how do you disrupt the status quo? Or, how do you align definitions of broken, or emblazon the perception that it really is on fire? While I'm not sure I can summarize that in 400 words, here are a few ideas:

First, keep looking for others who see things like you do. Finding an internal champion to harbor the idea and develop it on the inside carries a lot more weight than you do. *50,000 Greeks couldn't bring down Troy from the outside, but 50 from the inside could.*

People embrace the status quo because it largely requires little new effort. People are comfortable with things staying the same so don't fight it, celebrate it! Jill Konrath in her book *SNAP Selling* talks at length about how you should focus on your solution complementing their existing systems or procedures. It's worth a read.

Ask them probing questions. One I really liked from Jeffrey Gitomer's *Little Red Book of Selling* is: "How would you know if you were paying 20% more" than you should for something?[1] Questions like these capture attention because the action is on them to **reflect internally on what already exists**, not to consider an alternate path with you. Another way to capture attention is to change your outreach. Incorporating a video, using caps, bold fonts, mixed uppercase and lowercase all have ways to engage your audience. Just be temperate because employing these frequently makes you look unprofessional.

Remember (from *What Great Salespeople Do*) that: change is slow— we resist it. We attempt to rationalize the status quo (the ship is still above water) until we are forced to acknowledge that the status quo is untenable (my feet are getting wet!)[2]

Action Item: Only employ creative, "loud" tactics if your message is really worth hearing. No one wants to be remembered as the boy who cried wolf, so save these tactics for only the most extreme of savings or situations.

36. Tracks Ideal Timing/"Calendaring"(3 minutes)

In 2005, there was a song by Fort Minor called *Remember the Name,* and it broke down the 100 percent it takes to be successful. While I won't bust a beat right now with my sales *Remember the Name* remix, the point is interesting because one worth inclusion is luck (and timing).

Unfortunately, for many organizations, luck and timing are still about 50 percent of the successful sales organizational makeup. The problem with that is it's very conditional and hard to replicate. The reality of it is the vast majority of people and organizations aren't going to put forth a lot of effort into sales trainings and continued skill developments, so luck and timing is a reality; however, it doesn't need to be a complete crap-shoot. Here's how:

The reason why I've bundled luck and timing together is that with the exception of marketing qualified leads (MQLs) and bluebirds, people often confuse luck with timing. How many times have you heard about a prospect coming out of nowhere and wanting to learn more, include you in an RFP, get a proposal, and so on? I imagine more often than I originally imagined.

You can maximize timing with "calendaring" what's hot and when it's hot. Chances are your company has been around for a while and the experienced personnel know the semiseasonality of business. This isn't true for just retail, it's true for the vast majority of businesses—not all months are created equal. Hell, at Oracle, the month of May was about

35 percent of the total business and that's a software solution that can be turned on anywhere anytime!

My advice is to account for every product's spike in seasonality and **figure out your best lead time**. Choreograph with marketing to run events, trade shows, and webinars in that window so that you can be working symbiotically toward more business. This doesn't just maximize luck or timing, it maximizes productivity. How so? Because sending out Open Enrollment guides in April doesn't do much for 95 percent of the population, but it takes just as much time to do sending out in April as it does in October. I refer to this misstep as a "Christmas in March."

Everyone knows that Christmas is in December. Every year for as long as it's been documented, it's been in December. So, how would you feel driving people to come to a Christmas party in March? Probably not great. Why? Because it's a waste of time. No one cares about Christmas in March. Sounds simple and logical right? You're probably thinking, "Of course Alex—that's easy—I would never invite someone to a Christmas party in March." However, take a long look at your outreaches, How many Christmas' in March are you pitching?

Action Item: Get your company's monthly sales reports by product line for the past 5 years. Figure out your spikes in sales volume (factor in appropriate lead time for complex selling industries) and plan for a launch campaign 4 to 8 weeks in advance of that timeline. For any events, I'd say start inviting clients 3 to 5 weeks in advance to ensure calendar availability.

E-mail or LinkedIn me your 100 percent compositions of sales success! You can find the lyrics to *Remember the Name* at lyrics.com for inspiration.

35. Is Intrinsically Motivated (2 minutes)

I must say I chuckle while writing this one as I balance my time on a Friday at 11:49 pm writing this passage and juggling working on a finalist deck and event plan. I know, I know. I'm so cool.

While you may not have to work many Friday nights at 11:49 pm, you will need to work. A lot. And you will need to do things that no one asks you to do. No, this isn't my best attempt at work-related oxymorons; you will need to do things no one asks for. So, if following rules and the beat of someone else's drum is your tune, I wouldn't suggest sales.

What exactly do I mean by intrinsically motivated?

You're the type of person who's committed to her word, to giving it your best when no one is watching, and tending to the small details that others will say don't matter. You do not need a third party spurring you along with incentives, motives, or manipulations; **you do things because you want to be successful**, you're passionate about the pursuit of preeminence, and you cherish the path less taken.

Enough of me waxing poetic. Boiling it down, intrinsic motivation is to do it because you want to.

Action Item: Write down the 10 things you're most proud of. What do they say about you? What are the commonalities? Was it overcoming adversity? Good sign. Was it picking yourself up (see Ben's story in Simon Sinek's *Start with Why*)?

To take this one a step further, what are you going the extra mile to accomplish? Where does time fly by? What are you doing when you lose yourself smiling and churning out work?

34. Continuously Learns and Seeks To Better Themselves (2 minutes)

No one knows everything. Not da Vinci. Not Edison. Not your sales manager. And if you read my preface, not your professor. In fact, I've written 100 of these skills, and there are just about 25 that I'd consider myself an expert in. What's the point? It's that what *separates you from the rest is your consistent ability to improve yourself.*

Mark Manson in *The Subtle Art of Not Giving a F*ck* talks about how **those who are most successful are those who are relentless about their improvement**, and it stems from the fact they feel they aren't that great at all.

How can you start? Well, flip to the end of my book to see the 10 relevant books I've read to gain some insight on where they can be particularly helpful. Reading with an open mind is what I'd stress as vital. I wish I had additional perspective when going through my training at Oracle. My mindset was, This is one of the world's greatest tech sales companies, I will learn what they teach me. After all, it's best to do what they want, and I'll be successful. In the words of the self-proclaimed great Donald Trump, "WRONG." It's not about being a corporate soldier for your firm, and do not confuse expertise with universal applicability. You are best served getting input from a number of different sources and deploying the best tactics in the relevant moment.

Applying the Oracle playbook, no matter how masterful, has failed me and my team several times. If I knew other methodologies or trainings or applied other insights, I would have been better off. Moral of the story: READ READ READ! There is no one sales methodology bible.

Books are great, but I'm looking for other means! Blogs, online courses, company-sponsored trainings are all viable avenues. In fact, you might be surprised to see just how much your company wants you to learn, and resources like edX are available for you to master a skill (seems Negotiation is almost universally offered, and yet not many people are good at it). These are the ever-so important, immediate value adds, so take advantage where and when you can.

Action Item: Remember a few more words of Manson's: "the joy of the climb is the climb itself."[3] Read five more books than you would otherwise. Take notes and revisit the notes to help you in real time.

33. Learns and Loves Competitors and Differentiation (2 minutes)

Most of sales is about trying to find ways to stick out and be memorable; differentiate yourself, your company, and your process. We may think we are so different from others, but for all we know, we could be exactly the same.

Because we aren't privy to all the other e-mails, meetings, presentations, and proposals that others (namely our competitors) put together, it's hard to nail down if we really are standing out from the pack.

You can't begin to know if you're different until you do your homework on your competitors. How they advertise, language they use, product offering similarities and differences—you need to know it so that you can understand how they *maneuver* so that you can *outmaneuver*. Knowing your competitors well helps you with one of my top 10 skills (sneak preview time!) Pivoting. Let me share an example with you.

Working in inside sales at Oracle, I was extremely familiar with people trying to rush me off the phones. Oftentimes, I would encounter many an HR leader saying point solutions or incomplete suites like Cornerstone or iCIMS do everything for them. They think they can lump everyone into the same bucket because it's a great way to shut down the conversation in one fell swoop. Without knowing their suite of solutions, that would have been game, set, match. Fortunately, knowing what solutions they didn't offer allowed me to pivot to said solutions and pick up opportunities.

Knowing your competitors doesn't only serve you in the early prospecting stages. In fact, knowing your competitors can help you price, present, and probe; if you have a basis for the incumbent or the others competing for your client's business, you have directional indicators. In this way, knowing your competitors is your compass; without it, you're unsure of your course and the direction you're going.

Action Item: Run a win/loss analysis after a decision has been made. Once guards are finally down, this will allow you to learn more about exactly where you stood out or fell short. Record this information, as it is vital to your learnings and future opportunities. Study it.

Tools, savings, company history, and mission—they all run together. Point out the obvious to them so that they can not only follow along but also remember you.

32. Mitigates Self-Oriented Needs (Intelligence, Ego, Validation) (2 minutes)

Just the other day I was on stage in front of over 100 people speaking on a panel of many esteemed colleagues but noticed one flaw in multiple presentations—want to venture a guess? It was their need to feed their self-orientation.

The need to hear yourself talk, *the need* for an idea to be yours, *the need* for people to think you're smart: these are all items about you and showcase your self-orientation. As I declined to piggyback, echo, add to, or elaborate on that—I smiled thinking about David Maister's master (talk about an appropriate last name) piece *The Trusted Advisor* and his trust formula: Trustworthiness = Credibility + Reliability + Intimacy/Self-Orientation.[4] You can be tremendous at the first three, but if your self-orientation is high, your results will lack.

I know I said I'd save my endorsements until the end, but *The Trusted Advisor* is a must read for anyone in consultative, relationship-driven sales endeavors.

For those of you thinking you do a good job at mitigating self-oriented needs, how do you do at this excerpt from David's book?

× A tendency to relate their stories to ourselves
× A need to too quickly finish their sentences for them
× A need to fill empty spaces in conversations
× A need to appear clever, bright, witty
× An inability to provide a direct answer to a direct question
× An unwillingness to say we don't know
× A recitation of qualifications
× A tendency to give answers too quickly
× Closed-ended questions early on[5]

How many did you flag as being habitual? Frequent? Occasional? Sometimes, the key to making a change is knowing exactly what to look for, and perhaps, these nine will knock something loose for you to improve upon. Personally, I recognize my need to appear professional, especially in looking older and dressing up. While I warn against the dangers in skill

#100, I too often touch my hand to the stove knowing it's hot out of my love for fashion and dressing up.

If it sounds desperate or makes you look like a braggart, skip it. This isn't an intelligence competition, think of it more like a date, and like on a date, it is exceedingly difficult to start building a trusting relationship with a potential client by trying to convince them of all the rational features and benefits.

Action Item: Read *The Trusted Advisor* and give yourself a 1 to 10 scorecard rating on each bullet point for how you're doing in mitigating self-orientation.

31. Understands Parity and Shifts to the Compelling Unique (2 minutes)

Time is the most precious commodity there is in life, and it is not to be wasted or trifled with in any way. So, why do so many people waste time speaking about things that are 97 percent the same as their competitors? Whether it is an issue of competitive intelligence ignorance, presentation negligence, or shear "that's just what we do around here," this happens all too often.

Focusing on unaddressed commonalities with competitors brings up another issue: it reassures the prospective client that you are in fact the same as the lower-priced alternative. You had an hour to present and spent 40 minutes discussing the same things to the same degree with the same veracity as the lower-priced alternative? Welp, I guess you're at least 67 percent the same as them and that's good enough for me! Procurement will be happy I picked them.

Now like many things in this book, it sounds basic, and it is. However, talking about your differentiators is in fact itself—a differentiator. And no, I don't mean talking about your client service, size, experience, or any other generic, baseline statistic. Tangible, bottom-line impacts and quantifiable metric-driven track records of success are what you need.

If you're not sure you're hitting on things that are truly differentiated or not sure they are seeing the impact, call out a point of parity. Nothing jars people awake and out of the hum-drum doldrum(s) like saying (especially in a demonstration): You know Frank, this is pretty similar to what they saw with ABC competitor. If it's OK with you Lindsay, I'd like to make sure you see the real differences in what we offer, is it fine to proceed onto something else and we can revisit this to solidify your understanding of us completing your needs on this topic later on?

Things that will help you capture your audience's attention on the true differentiators—the compelling unique—are using words **like proprietary, different, advantageous, sole provider/resource**. People's ears perk up around these words because that's where your most immediate advantage for helping them lies.

Relationships take time, service delivery's proof is in the pudding, executive sponsorship is another nontangible factor that can only show with time. The concrete, tangible, drivers of differentiation are centered around those words aforementioned, and the more technical, statistical, or patented information you can show, the more people will want to engage.

Action Item: Where do you have the biggest advantages? Can you back them up with statistical, third-party data? How can you best summarize these points? How will you call them out (change in speaker, tone, pause, pace) to draw extra attention to these points?

CHAPTER 8

30 to 21: Winning Their Business

30. Builds, *Maintains, and Leverages* *Engaged Network*

First off, this one would be higher, but not everyone reading this book is 45 or older. Networks take time to build, engage, and leverage. Yet, it always seems the foundation is a little wobbly.

I know plenty of people good at building networks. Everyone is eager to get that feeling of satisfaction meeting someone new and collaborating on a business idea. Unlike just about anything else in life, the hardest part is maintaining it. Think about it—how many great initial conversations have you had with someone (who isn't a direct potential customer) and then poof—vanished? A lot, right? Worse yet, maybe you get a message from them a year later asking for something. Is that genuine? Not really.

Maintaining a strong network is about **consistently engaging with folks and NOT looking for something but rather giving, or offering, something of potential value to them**. Now this is difficult because not everyone you meet or every client you have will be able to/should be able to give back. And therefore, back to the onion I go; peeling layers.

At the central core of your onion should be your top clients and those you've done a lot for. The ones if you need something you wouldn't hesitate to ask. How many do you have in this sphere?

The next layer out would be those people you need to incentivize to help but would ultimately help you out. OK, tally those numbers.

Next up would be your give-to-get types: help them and they will help you. Just be careful that you aren't doing anything that forces an issue that looks like quid pro quo. How many do you have in this layer? Now, how many do you have total? These are your focal point few.

Your last two layers might not directly amount to much, but it's important to keep in touch, as they may appreciate hearing from you. In this fourth layer, you are most likely just keeping in touch, should an industry event pop up or time comes around where you can help them and vice versa.

OK, now finally, the outside layer. Aptly, this is that sort of greenish onion layer to signify your relationship is new or *green*. In this last layer, out are the people you're friendly with and you pass along details about to other people interested in them (potentially make an introduction), but it's not much more than that.

How many do you have here? How many contacts in these layers all together? Now compare this to your LinkedIn connections; how'd you do? How many fell into one of the five buckets? If you're saying 30 percent or more fell into one of these five (and you're being honest with yourself), you're off to a good start.

Action Item: Go through your LinkedIn every 2 weeks and see which connections you can send a message. I'd suggest doing this on Monday mornings or Friday late afternoons when your other work is relatively light. Birthdays are great for outer circle, job updates, and changes for the second layer in, events for the third layer in, and so on.

29. Gets Clients to Prioritize and Rank

There's no shortage of information to take in during a client discovery call. 27 questions later, you have a wealth of information, but how do you know if finding the lowest-priced vendor or the one with the best service delivery model is the top priority? Well, you ask. Earth-shattering, I know.

I was hoping I would not have to list this as a skill, but I'm afraid I do. And at #29, you realize how lacking this skill is. People run through their questions and use intonation, order, pitch, or repetition to indicate top concerns, KPIs, or focal points. Sometimes that's effective, but sometimes it isn't. Even worse, if you didn't take note of their body language or speech patterns, you likely forgot which topics came up more often. Provided your boss isn't the type to check in with you every day, you probably forgot, and guess what? You probably guessed. Uncomfortable? Yeah, so am I. It's tense just to type these words down.

After observing a number of sales leaders at Oracle, one colleague and friend of mine had a system I found valuable: he concluded each call with ensuring he got the prospect's priorities right. If they weren't given, he would ask for their top five priorities. Sometimes to encourage them to think and take the question seriously, he would offer up what he thought the top 2 to 3 were, ask how they'd rank those and ask for anything else? This **closes the call with clarity and ensures you're hitting the mark** (funny enough his name is Mark). While clients may not think much of this effort, it provides comfort that they were heard, and you will communicate clearly to your colleagues.

There are three other reasons why I'm particularly fond of employing this question at the end:

It

1. Gives you focus on what takes precedence, what to hone in on, and what to come back to.
2. Gets them on your side because you're talking about what they want, not what you want. Yet of course, it still serves your own interests.

3. Gives important direction to your (management team, boss, team):
   ○ If everything you're much better at than the competitors is a priority, you stand a better chance. If your strength(s) didn't make the top three or are at the bottom of the top five—you're in for an uphill battle.

Action Item: Take inventory of your top 10 strengths as a company in this particular product/solution area. Now take your 10 weakest points. How did their top five shake out? How many strengths? How many weaknesses? How many in the middle/in neither category? Utilize the hockey statistic of plus/minus to get your net score and plan accordingly for the deal.

28. Gives Concessions When Needed, but With Stipulations

One of the parts of the sales process that I find frightens many is negotiation. Salespeople are concerned—what kind of discount are they going to ask for? How far off are we? How much will we need to give up?

Notice a theme? They are all one directional comments—what will I need to do to get their business? Provided you are not selling a commodity, you should view this as a partnership, not as you selling them something (vendor), but rather you partnering with them to offer your expertise to solve their challenges (advisor). This partnership is a two-way street, and as such, if they want something, they should be offering something in return.

Now the most common ask is around a lower price. Provided you gave them 2 to 3 options, you've done your due diligence on comparing apples to apples and found out the reason for the ask, you'll now be wondering, what should I ask for in return?

#1 on your list should be **future work opportunities**. What other things are they looking to accomplish in your space and in what timeframe? If you're giving a 10 percent discount but have four other projects, you'll be considered for within the year, then you are off to a good start. Utilize this opportunity to find out more about the intended evaluations and who will be leading them. You've been given a gift—they are coming to the negotiation table (often signifying you are the, or one of the, top choice(s)) and asking for something. Be polite (often saying what usually helps my clients get the best deals is) but poised. This is your time to showcase how you're working to accomplish their goals and in order to get approval from Big Bad Management, here's what helps get the lowest price.

It's hard to get through every potential ask, but to round out your top five, I would say to ask about:

1. Reference-ability: Simply, will they agree to be a reference? Allow their logo to be shown in presentations? Do a video testimonial?
2. Referrals: Do they have other people they know are looking for what you have to offer? Can they offer an introduction to an executive colleague? An industry friend?

3. Contract Terms: Would they agree to a longer or shorter-term contract (whichever is better in your industry)? Are they going to agree to your standard terms and conditions? The cancelation clause?

4. Alternative Arrangements: If price is really challenging, will they agree to contingencies/shared savings? Employee or revenue growth contingencies? Guaranteed increases after the initial contract? Shared risk on performance guarantees?

Action Item: Negotiation tends to be an area of missed opportunity. I typically hear people talking about discounting their fee when another tactic would have worked. The saddest part is they often didn't even bother to ask. Use the aforementioned to be a simple guide, and for more, read *Negotiation Genius* by Harvard Professors Deepak Malhotra and Max Bazerman. Their tactic of logrolling (or negotiating multiple items at once) will help ensure some give/take with your client and take the emphasis off price.

27. Resolves Objections

One prevailing misnomer I see among sales leaders is this sense of the need to overcome or neutralize objections. This is not a hike up Mount Everest, and it's also not a military strike. We are not trying to conquer, overpower, or otherwise defeat our prospect's objections or need for clarifications. If someone is offering objections, they are testing the waters of comfortability. While they may seem hostile, assume positive intent and reframe (in your mind) their question as the following: This is a potential concern for me if we were to work together, how can you make me (more) comfortable with your solution? When you approach with this frame, you'll find your answers are much more care-full and understanding.

One thing I see even the sharpest consultants and strongest salespeople falling victim to is they will provide a clear, lucid answer and then move on. They knew the question would come up and they answered it clearly. Clear for them because this is the world they inhabit each and every day. But, was it clear for their potential client? We don't know! Why? Because no one asked!

Don't just think your amazing answer and their silence or their cessation of ping-pong question-paddling means you answered it clearly—ask! I find that seeking and **getting confirmation of clarification** goes a really long way. All too often we assume our points got across and move on or worse yet, our "does that make sense?" question is viewed as dismissive, arrogant, or assumptive.

What I find to be a great way to ask clients if their question is resolved is to ask: "Does that answer your question in full?" or "Does that fully address your concern?" If you think the person may be concerned about their image being adversely impacted by admitting that they are still unclear, assume your answer wasn't clear by either saying "What else can we address for you on this topic/what else can we discuss to get you completely comfortable with this solution?" or "I realize that doesn't fully answer your question, let me add". Use these sample probes as a starting point for what will work with your client.

Action Item: Get 3 to 5 probes for confirmation of clarification in your repertoire. No one likes being asked the same question every time they ask a question, so versatility is key.

Watch the client's body language during your team's answer in order to see when you should probe further. I would say to probe early in the conversation so that the client will feel comfortable raising their voice without your prompt later in the meeting. Look to probe no more than once every 7 minutes. That's a maximum of four probes in a 30 minute meeting. More than that and you're basically assuming they don't understand anything you're saying.

26. Gives Proactive Options

The rule of three states that things are inherently more attractive, satisfying, or otherwise effective when a trio of options are presented as opposed to other number combinations. Think about sizes; what does everyone have? S, M, L.

Think about famous groups and literary figures—Three Blind Mice. Three Musketeers. Three Stooges. Three is the most simplistic way to offer choice. From a number of angles, three seems to be the magic number. And yet, when we put together our pricing proposal or response to fees in an RFP, what do we so often do? Present one option!

People don't like one option. It's easy to say no to (which is not good for you), and it comes across as one-dimensional and/or pushy. For naysayers, it gives them the out to overrule others citing your inflexible approach and implicit lack of creativity. For those hopeful to get approvals for you, it doesn't give them much to move your proposal up the ladder. Something else keeping one from climbing the ladder is **one option is easy to get confused about**. Someone could easily misinterpret your structure, and before you know it, you're out of consideration without notice. Three Dog Night was right when they said "1 is the loneliest number."

It's easy to see the many potential downsides you need to protect against with just one option, but there's also a strong positive to presenting multiple options; *logrolling*. As defined in the book *Negotiation Genius*, "Logrolling is the act of trading across issues."[1] When you present three options with different subtle structure changes, you get to see what's important to your clients. On top of that, your negotiations and potential concessions are now broader than just price and discounts. Long story short, providing proactive options acts as the prelude or setup for logrolling.

Now I didn't label this section "Implement the Rule of 3" because I realize there are years of company history and layers of approvals above you/predating you that won't come around to not one, but TWO, more options! Therefore, your middle ground is two. Even having two options proposed opens up the door to logrolling and better showcases your flexibility as an organization and your commitment to working with them.

The best thing about providing proactive solution options is that it begins the negotiation process and often concludes the decision process. Think of the old, "do you want this in red or green?" example. You're beginning to make commitments to the structure of the deal which implies… you agree to a deal.

Action Item: Now an important distinction here, especially given the preceding car sales reference, do not jump the gun! If you're in relationship-oriented large sales, do not use these as closing techniques; it insults your buyers and damages long-term potential. For more about closing techniques and their viability, read *Spin Selling* by Neil Rackham.

25. Personalizes and Materializes Through Storytelling

Some people are auditory learners. Others are visual. Some are a combination of the two. You know what I've learned everyone is? An example learner. If you don't believe me, look at the report from Chip and Dan Health that found 63 percent of the meeting attendees remembered stories compared to only 5 percent remembering statistics. Powerful statistic (wish I could say the same for those presenting!); why is this the case?

Stories bring information to life. They provide real-world, tangible, connectable examples that summarize multiple key data elements easily. Because they are such a strong encapsulation of reality, people perk up their ears when they hear a story is coming and they lean in. From an early age, we've been conditioned to love stories. From story time at school, bedtime stories at home, or scary stories at camp, stories have been a constant point of enjoyment in our lives.

Stories (in the business world) aren't just vivid encapsulations of reality, they are also invitations to listen and lay back. Our brains are constantly working to differentiate and distinguish data and people; we are constantly thinking and sometimes even thinking about thinking. When someone starts a story, we avoid the tendency to do two things at once and **we avoid the inclination to call everything they say into question**. As Michael Bosworth discusses in his book *What Great Salespeople Do*, "We subconsciously tell ourselves, Oh, it's just a story. I don't have to do anything or decide anything. I can just listen and enjoy."[2]

The beauty of these observations is they aren't just anecdotal, experiential, or theoretical. They are scientifically proven. You can share thoughts without that seemingly ever-present sense of skepticism because stories activate our limbic brains. As Bosworth points out, "story is the antidote to the critical left brain, offering a pathway around the barriers we put up against people trying to influence us."[3]

Now storytelling is a big stage, and all eyes are on you when it comes story time. You may think that eyes are always on you, but they aren't. Sometimes, they are on their phones, their hands, their notebooks—or when they are on you, they can be aimlessly rested there as they day-dream or contemplate. But not during storytime. Storytime is your time to shine.

So needless to say, you need some tips. Here they are:

Action Items: Be poised; don't speak too quickly or be hesitant. People aren't inclined to respect you when you speak quickly or show hesitation. If you aren't confident in your own words, how are they supposed to be?

Don't correct yourself in the middle of your story multiple times, people will go back to what you corrected and linger there—they won't be following along once you move on in the story.

Don't underestimate the importance of practice. You want to be smooth and the only way to ensure that is to practice your main story points in advance.

Focus on what's important to them, and don't get hung up setting the stage. When you take a long time setting the setting, you indicate your inability to focus, you waste time, and energy on menial tasks, and this serves as a leading indicator as to how you would be as a business partner. Background and build are important but basics are not.

24. Asks the Tough Questions

Remember when I spoke about body language and the lady who after our presentation walked away from us toward the lunch room? (*Whispering* If you don't remember, it's skill #72) Great. Keep that story in mind.

The build up to that story may surprise you. You know how that meeting started? It started with our decision maker on her computer and twirling the curls of her hair. Clearly, she had a lot on her plate (and mind), and we weren't at the top of the list. Much to the dismay of my team, I stopped the opening of our presentation to ask: "Excuse me (Jane), do you need a moment to finish something up?" Taken aback by the frankness but polite tone and wording, she replied—"No, go ahead." And proceeded to close her laptop and begin engaging with us.

If you recall skill #72, you recall I ended it with saying I hadn't heard and I wasn't holding my breath. Well, there's a reason that's #72 and this is skill #24. That's because we just won their advisory relationship. Like just 5 hours ago.

If you've ever been in sales you know **the worst thing about an opportunity is knowing what you have to do and not feeling confident, empowered, or "controversial" enough to do it**. That's what I encountered with Jane. I knew I had a choice—continue with our expertly crafted presentation or stop and switch gears. We opted for the latter. And while our next three closest competitors were markedly less than us, we were the only ones who asked the tough, throat-clearing questions and adapted to her. It was a new topic for her and even after our most well-crafted messages, I was the one saying, "but does that really make you feel comfortable with the process? What would make you comfortable with a potential switch?"

Now these questions weren't too controversial, not like the categories of pricing, incumbents, approvers/ratifiers, challenging prior relationships, and so on. Many of those will require advanced preparation among the entire team. And, don't sell this part short! Sometimes answers to these questions are just as important as the entirety of the presentation. Don't be afraid to spend an hour crafting a reply to a top concern.

Action Item: Get in on the table! It is important to understand if you're approaching a skeptic, hypocrite, or pacified person, and play according to their styles. If you're worried these questions will ultimately jeopardize your relationship, then get someone else to ask! Ideally your +1 level executive/manager is the right person to get these sticky situations done. Plan these in advance—it gives your team ammunition and ensures a well-choreographed answer when the time comes. Nothing says reassurance like an executive alleviating your top concern absolutely.

23. Analyzes What's Working (Tracks Client Responsiveness)

"Unfortunately, we lost the notes on this portion of our sales strategy"

Figure 8.1 Lost sales strategy
Happens more Often than You Think

So often, early in my career, I heard about "Analysis Paralysis" and about how I should just hit the phones versus running different analyses they never considered. For any of my young readers, the way to overcome that objection is to do this on your own time—over the weekend or after hours and oh-won't-you-be-rewarded.

If you don't believe me, take it from perhaps the most iconic sales book of all time—*Spin Selling* by Neil Rackham. What did his analysis show? The two things that stood out about the best salespeople were review and dissection of meetings/calls and getting all details right.

In my own world, I realized just how important stopping to reflect on my successes was at Mercer. Formerly at Oracle, I was able to knock down doors until someone responded. 30, 40, 50, 60 messages in is what it took sometimes. At Mercer? Five. Maximum. If I did not hit them with something valuable, attention-grabbing, or timely, I was cast off into the either figurative or literal Blocked Vendor category. An analysis of my successful outreaches showed me that 95 percent of opportunities came from when I reached someone within my first five attempts; even if it was nothing more than a Thank You, let's stay in touch. 100 percent of sold opportunities came from responses within the first three outreaches.

This analysis let me work much more effectively on crafting strong, out-of-the-gate messages and on pivoting to a multithreaded approach in; if I couldn't get in the front door within my first five tries, let me contact the maintenance crew or front desk about getting a key.

Of course, managers want you to track your # of outreaches and follow-ups, but how are you doing at tracking:

- How multithreaded are you?
- How many outreaches until you're successful? Is there a minimum? Maximum? Time of day? Day of the week?
- What topics get responses? Are the responses positive? Negative? Neutral?
- What time of year are people more often getting back to you?
- What e-mail headers are working?

These are just five questions to probe you to think deeper about your approach. If something isn't working, try a different approach.

An important declaration—this isn't just for the prospecting stage either. Seeing how often (percentage of outreaches replied to), how quickly (minutes, hours, days?), and how proactive (after a lag they find me, I don't find them) your prospects are because these are some of the most important metrics in tracking a deal to close. All these metrics tell me where I stand, and/or more importantly, how much of a priority it is for them/ their company.

Action Item: Use these five questions as a guide. I'd recommend analyzing how multithreaded you have been on an account; you're likely to be surprised that you've only been trying one or two people and chances are there is a third or fourth to go to.

22. Humanizes the Client (Empathy: Not CFO, but Jack)

Be empathetic. Sounds strange to make this demand, but it's not really something you see in sales books or sales trainings. So what can you do? How does one become empathetic? What does empathy even mean? Empathy is *the ability to understand and share the feelings of another.* How can you share the feelings of another when people are unwilling to share? And if they are unwilling to share, how can you understand them?

Throughout this entire book, I talk about how people have their walls up and guards drawn. In addition to those ideas to get people to lower their guard (or for the aggressors—get them to lower their gun), there is one more key "ingredient." Michael Bosworth talks about this in his book *What Great SalesPeople Do*: "Vulnerability is a key ingredient—perhaps the key ingredient—to emotional buy-in, to cutting through the veneer of bullshit."[4]

In many difficult circumstances (take Bosworth's example of hostage negotiations), you see successful relationship developers and negotiators going first. Why? It shows others that it's OK to open up; I trusted you with this information about me—you can talk to me if you want. Vulnerability is real. And, in business, a lot of time is spent on what isn't real. Once someone has acknowledged and accepted this realness, they will share. Therefore, vulnerability alone has solved for half of our empathy equation.

To understand *and* share those feelings, you must treat people as people, not as roles. Get to know their life outside of work, note it in your journal, and mention it as it comes up or comes time for a friendly gesture. It's Jack, not ABC Company's CFO. Jack is a father of two boys who play Little League baseball and vacation in Cape Cod. Oh, and Jack happens to be the Chief Financial Officer.

The funny thing I notice when you treat prospects as people and not as those occupying roles is it **not only helps your relationship with the prospect, it helps your relationship with yourself**. It helps with your nervousness or your inclination to be obsequious. It's no longer the all-powerful CFO who you should tremble before! It's Jack. And while he should be respected, listened to, and appreciated, he walks on two legs just like you.

Action Item: Now that you have all the tools to understand and share the feelings of Jack, work on your body language and actions. Responding to someone's story with appropriate body language is almost as important as the word's you use. Keep that front of mind.

21. Does What's Right for the Client's Long Term, Not One's own Short Term

Five years ago, I was on a third round phone interview for becoming the first U.S. sales rep for an HR software company based in Europe. The VP of Sales was a very sharp guy who asked all the right questions and certainly proved he would be a great guide. The one question he asked me that really stood out was:

If you had to choose between selling a solution a customer did not need or missing your quota, which would you choose?

I realized the difficulty of the question and gave an in-between answer of breaking it into pieces to sell them only something they could benefit from and getting a portion of the deal. Not a bad answer I thought, and he let me proceed (and eventually get the offer) forward. Oftentimes, I'd think, what if I was forced to pick? Which would I choose? At Oracle, this would have been a tough answer. Now, I would gladly volunteer to miss my quota.

This is perhaps the biggest "I wish I learned this earlier" lesson in my career. I was the top salesperson in my division. I never missed a quarterly goal in my inside sales roles. Sounds great, right? Wrong. Often, I had to refer to pressure tactics, selling fear, hustling hard to make it. The fear of failure kept me living in the near term and made the long term all that more difficult.

It didn't manifest itself right away, but it did when I left Oracle for Mercer and thought, Who should I reach out to? Unknowingly, I was restarting my relationships with every promotion I got, and I wasn't able to keep in touch. I realized this mistake stemmed from how some clients probably felt like they'd been bullied or pressured into a sale. Long-term relationships I could count on two hands and clients who would gladly pick up the phone from me—the interested, helpful, responsive rep they had—about five. Not great for 4 years.

Jeffrey Gitomer has a great section in his *Little Teal Book of Trust* that talks about the six stages of being a salesperson. They are:

1. Salesperson
2. Consultant

3. Advisor
4. Strategic advisor
5. Trusted advisor
6. Trusted advisor and resource

Now you likely won't make it to Stage 5 or 6 very often, but how often do you even make it to Stage 2? Stage 3? **The further you can go down this funnel (as opposed to your pipeline funnel), the easier sales will be** as time passes by. Don't seek sales, seek opportunities for you to actually, legitimately, no immediate reciprocation expected, help people for the good of THEIR business in the short and LONG term.

Action Item: Don't worry about missing a monthly or quarterly quota so much; I wish I learned this earlier. Pursuing short-term gains at the expense of a long-term relationship leaves you constantly rebuilding your funnel as opposed to managing it.

CHAPTER 9

20 to 11: Standing Out as a Consistent, Top Performer

20. Summarizes Effectively (2 minutes)

Any sales presentation ever, what's your role? To open and to close. What do they share in common for skillsets? Summary. It's a short attention span world out there (as shown by the fact I'm writing 1 to 2 pages about 100 skills and incorporating over 25 different bestselling books) and you're the one who needs to keep it on track. How? Well, for starters, pay attention. Every word said, every gesture made; every hair curled, fingernail bit, toe tapped—you're responsible. Exhausting? Yes. But, it is your job.

Subject matter experts (SMEs) are there to go into detail about a client's issues and their SMEs are there to probe, question, and most of all, showoff. What happens? Meetings of eight people really turn into a 2 to 3-person side-stage Shakespearean soliloquy, and for many, just as confusing and off-putting too. What does this mean for their executive decision makers? Tune out time! What happens then? After they disengage, they will ask the SMEs for their input. Whomever checks the boxes for these (Miller Heiman) technical buyers at the lowest price—bingo! Deal signed.

This isn't even as bad as it can get. As opposed to shutting down their attention spans, they could get discouraged that they aren't following these long asides and discussions. Executives, like you as a consulting salesperson, are involved in many matters that require their versatility. Heck many of them were former salespeople themselves. Given demands for their attention, they could drift off to their smartphone. **Retain their attention span** and go a step further to engage them through summarizing key inputs. Do so in a manner that outlines your key points.

So, John (fellow *XYZ* company colleague), if I'm hearing you correctly, we can accomplish that in one of three ways. 1-*X*, 2-*Y*, 3-*Z*. We are recommending *Y* because of *A* and *B*. Did I capture that correctly? Anything you'd like to add for Joan (CxO) and Bob (CxO)?

If you're picking up what I'm putting down, you're starting to realize it's not you pitching in the first and the ninth and sitting in the dugout for innings 2 to 8. You're in there throwing a pitch an inning to keep everyone fresh and better yet, to keep your team ahead of the competition.

Action Item: Don't be bullshitting in the bullpen; be mindful on the mound. Discuss with your team where you can add value through summarizing in advance. If there are parts where technical buyers frequently go down the rabbit hole, have a plan for how to bring it back to the larger group and how to transition into the next topic.

19. Meets People in Their Own Skin and in One's Authentic Self (2 minutes)

Every quarter, we discuss events. Where should we invest? As lead sponsor or supporting? Cover more on smaller dollars or go all in on one or two? My answer was a surprising one recently: none of the above.

Now don't get me wrong, sponsorships can be great ways to get the word out about your company. If you're doing well but your brand recognition isn't what it should be, go for it. For us, as the perennial #1 HR consulting firm, I lobbied against it. Why? Because when you sponsor an event, people are aware and they meet you as their guarded self. They keep their distance, they skew or misinterpret your words to appear slick; they avoid you.

Let me paint you a picture:

You're walking to work and are approached by someone gesturing and speaking in your direction. Your headphones are on so you have the opportunity to look away and keep walking if you want to. If the person is holding a clipboard, what do you do? Probably keep walking. Now if that same person, dressed the same way approaches you in the same manner without a clipboard or lanyard around their neck; do you stop? Probably more often than the former. It's the same principle with sponsoring an event; you can meet people in their authentic self more naturally as an attendee than as a sponsor.

Now some of you may say well if they do approach me and want to know more, I have an immediate hook into their potential business.

Perhaps that's true, but more than likely you'll be talking about your company (self-oriented) and yourself (arrogant and boring); two topics that no potential buyer really wants to hear much about. Meeting someone organically removes those barriers and has a sort or originality everyone looks for, as evidenced by the fact that people try desperately not to meet their spouse on a dating app. Why? Because it lacks the spontaneity that gives life its extra meaning.

Long story short: Rather than bet on the potential prospect's ability to understand your situation and business perspective, wouldn't you rather **bet on yourself as a conversationalist?**

Action Item: Look into speaking as an expert or attending an event as a member or practitioner. Don't worry about being "found out"—It's not deceptive unless you make it so. Be honest about what you do when asked. Don't sell! Not in the first meeting and not on your initial follow up. Don't ruin the work you put in! A bodybuilder doesn't ruin his diet with poutine, and a senator doesn't ruin his campaign with public intoxication. Be steadfast.

18. Creates Immediacy (2 minutes)

Figure 9.2 Default—Ignore

I'm not going to beat around the bush on this one—it's difficult to create immediacy. Why? Because people want to do things on their own time. While people are becoming better at being open to ideas, a timeline is a different story. It's one thing to bring up something you think is valuable, but another to tell me when and how to live my life! The chasm here is that people view timing as something inherently theirs, it's on one's own terms. Yet when sales personnel try to create immediacy, they focus on themselves and the reasons why the buyer (who is also thinking timing is relative to themselves) should do the deal are neglected. I guess it is fitting that immediacy has two *I*s because it does in real life too: the salesperson's "I" and the buyer's "I."

Much like our political party system, it's hard to get people to overcome their own viewpoints and work proactively toward a common goal, so my advice would be to get/utilize existing information you have from your prospect to create a timeline.

When did they say they wanted to have a solution in place? What was driving that date? What drives them personally and professionally? Leverage whatever information you have or can get to **build a timeline that showcases their needs and get buy-in**. Work backward from this timeline to showcase all the steps involved and why the time is now or soon to get started. Once they've bought into the full timeline, see how well they adhere to each individual checkpoint; this will help you determine how serious their interest is.

Now, how do you reach those who won't buy into a timeline or are too close to the finish line to let them fade away now? Sales people and managers are particularly good at leveraging discount strategies and time-bound offers; however, these have their time and place. Much to the chagrin of many, time and place mean the opposite of anytime, anywhere. As Simon Sinek would advise, you should minimize your use of manipulations (discounts, promotions, fear-selling, etc.). If you can employ another way, whether that be relational or strategic, I'd advise those alternate means.

For the times you need to employ the small manipulations, first ask: Is it worth it? Those actions will carry long-term repercussions and will persist the "what are you offering for X behavior?" mentality. Not to mention, it will subtly change their viewpoint of you. Perhaps now you will never fully reach the "trusted advisor and resource" role and can only strive for "strategic advisor" (which is still fantastic). If you make the "Go" decision to use manipulations, have someone else do it—your manager or director are the first two I'd advocate so it doesn't get in the way of your direct relationship.

Action Item: For alternate "immediacy creators," consider getting industry experts and clients to play up the need for acting now. Is there a whitepaper or blog from an expert on why now? Is there a client in a similar industry who can pull them over the fence?

17. Overcomes Inertia (2 minutes)

Just like its cousin, creates immediacy (noted on the prior page), overcomes inertia is one of the trickiest skills to master in sales. I myself would self-grade at roughly 5 out of 10 on overcoming inertia, and it is one of my greatest focal points right now.

Overcoming inertia is the continuation of disrupting the status quo for those thinking back to skill #37. Disrupting the status quo is focused on your initial eye-opener to get people interested in discussing your idea; however, overcoming inertia is taking things from pursuit down through the funnel and into the win column.

In order to get your team the W, you will have to start small to get things in motion. A powerful example of starting small is in Cialdini's Book, *Influence* and the example of the American POW's who felt they betrayed their country. The Chinese started small with asking them to point out the small things that could be better in America. They got their subjects to write down these complaints. An incremental build got them more vehemently behind their disapproval of these bad things in America until what they were writing looked like they hated America.

Now, I'm not telling you to convince employees that they hate their employer, but the idea of getting their buy-in begins with the improvements they'd make. That will get the ball rolling. In order to prevent panic at them subjugating their current system, embrace the status quo.

Author Jill Konrath in her book *Snap Selling* discusses the importance of being viewed as a complementary solution to what they have in place. By pointing out all the things that can remain in place, the more comfortable your potential buyer is with embracing your solution.

Now starting small and embracing the status quo are two big change agents, but they will fall short unless you are presenting these ideas to powerful agents of change.

Agents of change, aka influencers and/or champions, are crucial to your success. After all, any outsider can present a compelling need for change, but at the end of the day, it directly benefits the said outsider. If you are going to truly overcome inertia, you need to empower a powerful voice inside the company to carry the torch for you if you want to see the finish line.

Action Item: What small building block foundation questions do you have to enable change? Are they trite and common? How can you develop your questions to ensure they are well-received?

Read Robert Cialdini's *Influence: Science and Practice.*

16. Adopts the Client's View (2 minutes)

For the first 2.5 years of my career, I was dumbfounded at how short-sighted, ignorant, and careless my buyers were. After all, my product had a clear ROI, was the best-of-breed, had a spider-web effect on the rest of the company, and oftentimes, had immediate or short-term savings. Yet, I received many Nos and many dragged, then eventually, stopped, feet.

All of us have had this thought at one time or another and even when we try to put ourselves in our client's situation, we are merely wearing the client hat but not embodying the client mindset. We discuss the 2 to 5 most common objections they might have and then anything beyond that—we just chalk it up to ignorance is bliss or they were too difficult anyhow.

It wasn't until Erica Volini put a spotlight on HR as a decision maker that I got it.

Erica took the stage and approached a topic few do: why people don't buy. Yawn. Boring. It's a room chalk full of salespeople AND potential BUYERS!! Erica was very skillful in her presentation. She one by one picked off all the reasons people don't do business and decide to remain with the status quo. I went from close-minded to eye-opened during her presentation and ended with shock that any of these ignored, lifetime chair-at-the-table seeking, disregarded "cost centers" ever rose to the challenge of implementing change.

Moral of the story? Peel back the onion and use more than logic. As Bosworth will tell you, people operate from emotion and use logic to justify their decisions; it's more emotion than logic!

Ask yourself:

- What are they fearful of?
- What don't they understand? Why don't they understand it?
- What are they doubting?
- What might they think is a point of parity?
- Where are they bored?

If you seek to understand their point of view as opposed to ignore or overcome it, you'll find yourself with a lot more closed, long-term business. Don't get caught up on right or wrong and fair versus unfair—this will get you nowhere. Many of my best pursuits, best presentations, best prospecting resulted in nothing because I approached, led, with logic. Do not ignore emotion. Embrace it.

Action Item: Be empathetic. Truly put yourself in their shoes. No bitching and complaining about their personality because while that may help you explain a loss, it doesn't help you gain a win.

15. Masters the Art of Not Caring (3 minutes)

One of the surprising truths I've seen across many sales books and articles is the sales paradox of all paradoxes: the less you care, the more you sell.

Now I realize a lot of you will be saying, well what about the skills of hard-work, genuine interest, empathy, and more? Aren't those in direct opposition to this sales skill/paradox?

The answer? Not really. As David Maister, Charles Green and Robert Galford describe in their book *The Trusted Advisor*: "Success comes to those who don't make success their primary goal."[1] To paraphrase, success comes to those who work hard to do the right thing. The right action for the customer's long-term benefit, the right thing for the sales process, the right thing by doing your homework in advance—the list goes on.

Once you've reoriented your mind that making the sale is not the marker of success/the end goal, you'll see a pressure lifted. A pressure that was squeezing you so tight, it was palpable to others, especially your clients. That pressure makes you look weak, desperate, inconsiderate, contradictory, overly emotional, pushy, quickly (and overly) attached, and fearful.

Now reorienting your mind is much easier said than done. You've got a family to feed and bills to pay—how can you suddenly stop caring about closing the deal? It's a boring answer, but you focus on each step of the sales process and how you can differentiate, overdeliver value, and build a relationship. **You can't truly build a relationship if the goal is the deal.**

To make an analogy, think of golf. In order to have any success at all, you must hit the ball. A simple concept, but there's more to it. If you notice the best golfers do not simply aim to hit the ball—if they did, their swings would look like chopping at a tree or playing croquet. A golf swing does not stop at impact, in fact impact itself is at about 70 percent of a golfer's swing. The follow through and finish have the bigger impact on success. Think of closing a deal in the same light—it's 70, perhaps 80, percent of the way there and the end goal is becoming a trusted advisor. When you start serving as a trusted advisor as opposed to a closer, you'll have greater success.

Now, a surprising thing happens when you stop focusing on "deals," you close more of them. While we may all say we want to help people out in tough times, the reality is we want to be confident in our decision and to be a confident buyer, we need to work with a confident, poised, seller. Someone who doesn't need our business means he or she must have a lot more of it coming through, and if they have a lot more, the solution must be worth it. Now I want it too.

Action Item: If you're having trouble getting in the carefree mindset, block your calendar for other activities, so you're not too available. Extend this a step further by playing "The Game" of being extremely responsive but not being too available. Get back to people quickly but with staggered time availabilities.

For my fellow perfectionists struggling to let go of the result, take the following passage from Mark Manson to heart:

The Ticket to emotional health is eating your veggies. The bland and mundane parts of life show that your actions actually don't matter that much in the grand scheme of things and that's ok. The constant pressure to be something amazing will be lifted off your back. This… will actually free you to accomplish what you truly wish to accomplish, without judgment or lofty expectations.[2]

14. Shows a Genuine Interest (2 minutes)

I remember one night feeling stuck on a prospect reachout; a small to midsized company in horse racing. I had nothing in common with their executives—no shared connections, no strong bonds, they weren't past clients or close to others who were, they didn't demonstrate any significant need via our public brokerage filings nor any engagement with our Marketing (Marketo) automation tools. I thought to myself, well I do really like horse racing and know a lot about how to bet based on fundamentals. Novel approach I thought and while it does not create immediate value, it was... different. Probably not something a CEO and CFO would want to hear about.

Wrong.

Within 10 minutes on a Monday night at 7 pm, I got a reply from the CEO who shared a similar personal story to me and asked to set up a meeting at his office.

That week I applied the idea to two other potential clients: one that managed my girlfriend's childhood residential community and another that was a charity I believed in and supported. Both I told my **personal story and connection to them**. Both times I got responses back to set up meetings.

There are so many people knocking down doors via blunt force, some with finesse, some with value, and many with savings, but there are few going in with a personal connection, belief, tie or, most importantly, *interest in their success*. Helping them turn a profit or recognize savings is nice but it's impersonal. At the end of the day, you can tweak that same message to 5 or 50 others. But, that's not the case here because these examples connect to people's emotional brains.

Now a word to the wise, don't overestimate how many differentiated, personal connections you have to prospects. In my territory of 200, it was a total of three. How do I know? The forced ones didn't work. The—oh I banked with you when traveling recently to Europe—didn't work. The I love your shirts and style of your brand—didn't work. Why? It was generic. And while true and a personal connection—it wasn't differentiated. Millions of people love the Yankees, so don't think your story about watching them on TV last night is going to get you in the door. As a matter of fact, lame, forced attempts like that last one may actually do more harm than good. It's greasy. You're trying too hard to connect with me on something you know little to nothing about. Ick. Stick to something poignant, powerful, and (a)propos.

Action Item: Research what each of your companies does. Do you have a connection to it? How strong is it? Ask someone else if they think it's unique or generic? Does it sound forced? Take your time. You get few chances to connect.

13. Offers Assistance Outside Own Company (2 minutes)

In a world where the need to avoid self-orientation and self-promotion is very high, nothing says you're here to help more than offering help outside your own company's offerings. Something along the lines of, "I was looking at your 5500 filing or annual report and noticed X issue, have you looked into solutions to solve X problem? **While it's not something my company does, I do have** (expertise/years of experience, connections, etc.) **who may be able to help.** Someone who looks to solve high value problems for me is someone I'm certainly interested in hearing from more and someone who has the opportunity to gain a life-long relationship with me, regardless of the company they represent or product line they sell.

If you have expertise in an area your company doesn't offer: perfect. Start there. While any help outside your own company's suite of solutions is good, ideally you'd offer assistance in something correlated to your solutions (if you sell HRIS software, recommending background screening providers may be productive) or at least to the same technical buyer (HR/HR Tech in both examples).

Another great place to look is into introducing common executives to one another. If you have a sponsorship or free membership to offer, do it. Let me share a story with you.

It's no secret that tons of people are reaching out to CFOs PITCHING. Cognizant of this issue, I wanted to find a different approach, so do you know what I did? I connected them with a membership body designed specifically for CFOs to collaborate and grow. While this was something outside my day to day, I found value in the organization, and so did several others. I'm not saying this is the end all, be all (as many still didn't reply), but for those who did, it made me credible, reputable, and trustworthy. For one particular CFO, it made me the trusted advisor so much so that she recently asked me "When (what time of year) should we switch to Mercer?"

Action Item: Develop partnerships—you may look like a hero and also get people to feel obligated to you. Even better yet—there might be a revenue share arrangement.

12. Demonstrates Resilience (3 minutes)

At Oracle, I participated in helping outgoing seniors/incoming workers decide their career path. One of the questions I got most often was, what do you need to be successful in sales? I think the answer surprised some people, but it was resilience. Why? **Because it's the skill you'll need most often.** You can always learn and get better but without bouncing back after a tough loss—you'll never even open your mind to growing.

The tough truth to face is that sales is about 5 percent highs and 95 percent grind. Before some of you get too disenchanted, I don't mean that you're climbing out of a dark cave for light 5 percent of the time. A more apt analogy would be a rollercoaster ride. If your highs and lows in sales are minimal but you have an exhilaratingly fast ride in the middle, that's perfectly fine. After all, life is about enjoying the ride itself, not just its peaks.

In order to ensure the ride itself is enjoyable, shift your perspective to ensure you aren't being stuck on small lows (e-mail not received, poorly aligned prospect saying no, comp plans not being what you want, office politics) and don't just save the highs for the mega-wins. Enjoy the breakthroughs and relish the small wins.

If 5 percent sounds too small to you, let me give you an entrée into one of the best mindset and perspective books there is, *The Subtle Art of Not Giving a F**k*. Manson comments that "For many of us, our proudest achievements come in the face of the greatest adversity. One must suffer emotional pain to develop greater emotional resilience, a stronger sense of self, increased compassion and a generally happier life."[3]

Why is this important? It's because starting out will be challenging, your lows will often outweigh your highs, but your highs won't mean anything unless you have lows. Life is relative, and if everything were easy and just pure bliss all the time, then you will feel like you haven't accomplished anything.

One of the most important elements is to realize you should let your downs get to you. Life is tough, embrace it so that you can move forward. Don't let the anger build. Let it out and move on. It happens to everyone. My personal biggest "That bites" moment was when I had a client give us the official green light. That official green light took place after nine approvals. NINE. The ninth approval came late in the evening after the CEO had left, but he was guaranteed to sign in the morning. To everyone's dismay, their key client (and 40 percent of their revenue) e-mailed them later that night saying they were terminating their relationship with my client.

My call the next day? Never mind no deal, I had to console the lady crying on the phone that she was being let go. Those. Those are lows. Take a break and recognize this is a confined, nothing you can do circumstance. Confined it was—it hasn't happened in six years since.

Action Item: Read Mark Manson's *The Subtle Art of Not Giving a F**k.*

11. Has a Long-Term Memory (2 minutes)

Can I share a story with you? (Hopefully you said yes. If you said no, you can skip to skill #10).

Last Christmas (insert musical humming here), I was sending out holiday cards thanking clients for their business. However, I took it a step further and wrote cards to my favorite former clients at my prior company. Sure it was 2+ (most of which 4+) years ago, but I didn't care. They were people I genuinely liked and wanted to spread good holiday cheer to.

Most of my outreaches went unnoticed by my current clients (par for the course for a dedicated, thoughtful account manager), but for the prior clients? A particularly warm reception. People genuinely shocked and happy to hear from me; I reached out to them even when I wasn't in a position to directly gain from them anymore. One result was particularly memorable.

A CEO I helped launch his training program by purchasing our software solutions (what most would say is the ideal win–win) responded with more than a Thank You. He responded with a job offer.

So impressed that I took the time to acknowledge our partnership together some 4 years ago, he noted the lasting impression it made on him and how he thought that attention to detail and ability to make people feel special was so worthwhile for the next phase of his company's growth, he offered me a Sales Director role. Something that even if I never take, I will always recall fondly.

What's my point? My point is to have a long-term memory. Amazing work done 5 years ago is great, but amazing work done 5 years ago brought to the forefront of memory with a sentimental touch is better.

It's the perfect way to show you're here for their long term and you care about them as a person, not a buyer or influencer. **You go the extra mile—you invest in relationships**.

Action Item: Track birthdays (client and their family members), favorite vacation spots, any other special days in their life. Reach out when it is most authentic. If you're expecting a decision on a major piece of business, perhaps hold off. You don't want your ingenuity and authenticity questioned when going the extra mile.

Bonus: Read the Mackay 66 Question Framework and extract the questions that will give you maximal bonding and rapport impact.

CHAPTER 10

10 to 1: Being the Trusted Advisor

10. Builds Advocates, Not Satisfied Clients (2 minutes)

After working at Oracle for over 4 years in a variety of positions, I had developed/harbored a certain amount of disapproval for Workday and its sales tactics. And here I was joining a firm that, when implementing HR software, only does Workday. Needless to say, I needed to open my mind. After all, they had always done well: if only I could figure out why...

Within the first 2 weeks at Mercer, I was sent to a Workday conference hosted by a Higher Ed client of ours in NYC. When I got there, I noticed a different sense of camaraderie; a sense of belonging and guards down. Impressive but still not enough to justify mid-market price tags of (at the time) 1.5 to 3x that of Oracle's. Then, Q&A happened. Some sharp prospective workday clients would ask probing, under-the-covers questions of Workday's sales team; the kind that would cause 85 percent of salespersons to perspire. What happened? How did he respond? He didn't say a word. And no, I don't mean he was so nervous he passed out or stammered incomprehensibly. Before he could say a word, two different Workday clients answered for him about how much they loved A, B, and C. Dee too. She's so responsive.

Game. Set. Match.

Workday had created a community of passionate practitioners that Jill Rowley would have been proud of.

Jill was one of the very first presenters I encountered in my professional career and one of her mantras (beyond UVA's Battle Cry Wa-hoo-wa!) was how she always sought to **build advocates, not merely satisfied clients**. Sounded great, but at the time, it was the sort of memorable marketing buzz phrase I jotted down without an idea how to actually, practically, see this through. Here at the Workday Higher Ed conference, I saw its byproduct firsthand.

But how exactly do you build advocates? Well, like many things in this book, it's a combination of various other skills. My advice would be to reference skills #2, 3, 5, 16, and 21.

Action Item: Read those skills intently! Remember Simon Sinek's building a cathedral or cementing rocks example? Apply that idea—are people passionate about what you do for them? Is what you offer a notable skill for their current job? Can it be promotion worthy? Career-enhancing? Find the common ground with your clients of how something is beneficial to them. I remember seeing speakers who were always eager to speak at Oracle's HCM World. Why? It was a stage in front of 2,000 people for them to demonstrate their expertise. Don't forget that. These people are building careers as you are building revenue streams. The main point to remember; *The Best kind of selling is the kind you don't have to do at all.*

9. Gets Help (2 minutes)

When your sales manager offers or insists upon helping, what's your response? You probably thank them for their offer, recoil in fear, and then never follow up on their offer. Why? While we may tell ourselves it's because they are a hindrance, it's likely because you're fearful of their involvement either because you feel you're in the proverbial hot seat or you're concerned they may have something negative to say to you or... to the prospect!

Fact of the matter is, if your management team can play a value-added role, they should. While you may think it ushers in unwelcomed opinions and fears, it actually mitigates them. A second pair or eyes and ears gives you twice as many vehicles to pick up on signals and twice as many hands to take note.

For those of you with superhuman hearing and typing abilities, I have reasons for you too. Think of the difficulty someone has in saying no. Now multiply that by 2x or 3x. Do you see them still so ready to give a resounding No? Probably not. Don't believe me? Think of the last time you had a special request at a retail store and someone had to get their manager to help—did you buy it? Say they needed to phone the owner—did your purchase rate increase? Probably did. We aren't so different from our buyers.

This external battle is one we have focused on throughout this book but, how about the internal battle? Getting help showcases your ability to look into all avenues to make something successful. That undying determination goes dually noted on your management's mind. It also gives you the opportunity to showcase your abilities. If they see your effort and your ability to turn each stone effectively and efficiently, then guess who is now shielded from negative repercussions? You are. They bought into the situation and you were just unlucky, whereas your teammate who could have done the exact same things and didn't involve management is now at risk of being called to the hot seat.

How do you put this into action? **Introducing executive sponsors into the proposal or presentation** is one way. If space is a constraint, I like to send an intro video or advance e-mail from/featuring said executive sponsor. One of the best, little more aggressive ideas I saw was from Jill Konrath's *SNAP Selling*:

"As soon as he feels he has a 50 percent chance of getting the business, he drafts a stellar letter for his CEO/COO to send his prospects."[1]

The important piece to remember is the further up the ladder you go, the more important having an executive on your side to mirror the prestige the client is bringing to the table. As Lee Salz describes, *CEOs want salespeople who have the ability to reach executive channels for resolutions.*

Action Item: Don't think of it as needing help, but as situations where getting help will differentiate you.

8. Tailors to Client Industry, Needs, Challenges, Egos (3 minutes)

One prevailing paradigm that I'm noticing now is—*generic never works*. You may have gotten hits on mass e-mail campaigns 3 years ago, but how are they working now? Probably not as well. Every successful salesperson I know tailors to a group, speaks their language in their desired tone, and drums up interest by getting group buy-in and utilizing that buy-in to build momentum. If there's any one sentence that sums up a salespersons role in this book—the preceding may be one to circle and circulate.

Where do you start? I'd say the low-hanging fruit is personalization. Think about the e-mails you open—if they say your first name, do they have a higher chance you'll read them? Probably. We aren't as difficult to connect with as people may think. We actually want to see people be successful because chances are you think you're pretty successful or good at your job and you like to see others who put forth the effort. Now a name isn't enough. After you personalized their name, company, and one timely/resonant item, you are proficient in personalization.

What's next? Following blogs and publications that speak the language of your buyer. For consulting, law, tech, and financial services, this process is well developed and fairly easy to make marked improvements to your messages quickly. For areas like private equity (PE) and insurance, it's a bit more complex and in the weeds. However, knowing the initial lingo can get you far, and it only takes one to build a village.

For PE, subtle changes can get you in the door. Instead of using the word "savings," talk about 3 to 7 percent EBITDA improvements. Talking about higher revenues may be good, but profits per partner in the law firm world is even better.

An important note here (even in e-mail!!) is it's not just what you say but it's how you say it. Super formal, buttoned-up e-mails with regards and salutations to start-up tech firms aren't cool and vice versa, the casual sign-off "Dash, First Initial" may not be appreciated by your 200-year-old banking prospect. This isn't too hard to decipher—look into the language on their website and the person's LinkedIn to get a feel for a proper tone. If I'm painting broad strokes, I'd say find a way to cross-pollinate conversational and creative with polite and poised.

Now that you've **personalized your resonant messaging in the language and tone of the buyer,** the feather in your cap is leveraging social proof points from the buyer's industry or role to showcase differentiated value. Once you've crafted something that is 90 percent of the way there, give it a go. After all, a 100 percent perfect intro message isn't worth the incremental lift in time and effort for something that isn't likely to get read the first time around.

Action Item: What industry languages do you speak? And at what level (Beginner, Intermediate, Advanced, Fluent, Native)? Write them down. What industries should you be learning based on your total addressable market?

7. Teaches Something New and Valued (2 minutes)

"This better be important."

Figure 10.1 What Your Prospective Client is Thinking

There are a million salespeople out there trying to get your prospects attention, how are you rising to the top?

Pointing out that Applicant Tracking Software (ATS) can cut time to hire or HRIS systems centralize and automate data isn't groundbreaking, and it's likely not getting you many returned calls. However, they may not know that many ATS providers have ways to capture tax credits for making qualified (veteran, disabled, etc.) hires. Others may not realize that HRIS systems can offer solutions in the finance space and planning and budgeting world too.

Point being if you get your prospective client to utter an adaptation from *The Challenger Sale* of "Huh I never knew that or I never thought of it like that"—you may be well on your way to a meeting.

Value is a tough one as its one of those words so commonly, and loosely, used that its meaning has become diluted. On top of that, value is a personal feeling; it's what someone gets after learning about, or the actual delivery, of a solution. So, it's hard to say something will be valuable to the individual person you don't know too well yet.

How do you teach something of value? You don't call it value or valuable. Words like different and alternative seem to garner more interest. While they may translate in your mind as the same thing, they often do not to the client. By saying you're unique, you're in fact common. By saying you provide value, you're actually a waste of time. The key is to get to questions surrounding their personal, and their organization's, success metrics. **Knowing how someone is incentivized will begin to show you what value is to them.**

Other ways to be valuable? Referencing similar clients, industry challenges, legal updates, and so on will help. If you can showcase ways you think outside the box and with their success ahead of your own, you're likely to succeed.

Action Item: Read Jeffrey Gitomer's *The Little Red Book of Selling* for some great ideas on how to connect with clients in "valuable" ways. One of my personal favorites is to schedule a dinner with a prospective client and introduce them to either a valued partner or someone who is interested in their cause or company at that dinner.

6. Pivots Effectively (3 minutes)

How often do you prepare for an introductory meeting by researching the prospective buyer's company, persona, and past dealings, look into potential synergies, cross all your T's and dot your I's only to find out that none of what you prepared is what they want to discuss? Pretty often right? It's the professional analogy to the dreaded—I studied all the wrong material for the test—syndrome we suffer from as children and young adults.

Now I realize that agenda-setting and other level-setting techniques can help mitigate this preparation frustration, but it's inevitable that in first meetings, conversations can be like herding cats. You want your prospect to feel heard, important, and to know you're aligned with their goals. But this is an opportunity to evaluate potential business partnerships together, and therefore, you have to get the conversation back on track, but how?

The simple buzzword is you need to *pivot*. For any basketball fans, you know the value of a low post forward backing down his opponent to have a sudden pivot, drop-step and bank off the glass shot for 2 points. While we shouldn't be looking to back down our conversation partners or necessarily overpower them, the concept is similar—you're going in one direction that is a low percentage chance of success and rerouting your direction and energy to find something more opportunistic.

Pivoting is especially important early on in sales cycles. While yes, you may need to change direction on the fly in finalist meetings to connect to your buyers, pivoting is most often employed when you are still getting a feel for your prospect and looking to artfully cover as much ground as possible. In cold calling or e-mailing, rarely does the first thing you say end up being the conversation. In fact, 80 percent of my deals at Oracle were from pivots. Someone is happy with X for Talent Acquisition software? Tremendous—one less thing on their never-ending list of needs. How about areas that X vendor doesn't offer, like handling the performance appraisal and feedback process?

Now, pivoting isn't easy. My advice is to think about how to bridge conversations. For example in HR, certain buzzwords are versatile like "engagement" and "effectiveness." Others like incentives, transformation, and innovation can open up doors as well. These words can help you subtly transition your way into another topic.

For hard-to-corral prospects who go off on deep tangents, think about how to **effectively summarize their statements, connect the dots, and offer paraphrased synopses that help steer in your direction.**

For example, if they said they had trouble with people attending their development sessions and open enrollment seminars, you may offer up that employee engagement in their current environment needs improvement. It's not the words they used, it's not a lie, and it builds "yes'" toward getting back on track.

Action Item: What are your pivot buzzwords? What words arise in everyday (your field) conversations that segue nicely into an area of differentiated value for you?

5. Employs Active Listening (3 minutes)

When you think about the working world, you ever realize how much time you spend repeating yourself? Any client service issue requires escalation up the chain and restating your case often. Any meeting inevitably has a project leader repeating themselves at the beginning. Sometimes, this is the nature of the beast, but most of the time, it's because someone failed to listen earlier on and/or failed to inform the rest of the team/meeting constituents of what was discussed.

It's disheartening to have to repeat yourself in each meeting and even more so when you have to do it in the meeting! Why does this happen so often? Well, for starters, it's because, typically, most people aren't *listening*. Instead, they are *waiting to speak*. They stopped talking so that you can say something before they say the next thing on their mind; they were extending this tiny courtesy to you—some don't even do that! They just babble on without letting you get a word in.

When you actively listen, you put your agenda to the side (showcasing you're mitigating your self-orientation) and let them become your focus. You have a dialogue as opposed to mindless chatter, and it's from there where you can see people open up. They open up because they feel heard, appreciated, respected, and feel like you're actually working toward improving their situation. You are sowing the seeds of trust while concurrently getting them to drop their salesperson shield or account rep armor.

One of my favorite encapsulations of "active listening" comes from Michael Bosworth's book, *What Great SalesPeople Do* and his mention of a certain Chinese symbol.

The Chinese symbol for listening contains **eyes, ears, undivided attention, and a king**. Why? Because you listen with both your ears and your eyes as you observe their words, prosody, tone, rhythm, and match that with what their body is telling you. Your undivided attention is on them (it's not on your phone, your watch, your pen), and by having this locked in, captivation on them, they feel special—like a king. Now it's important to be locked in without being locked on. If the client or prospect feels like they are being watched like you'd watch television or it appears you're fixated on them, they may recoil citing you're coming across as overeager. This is why, it's important in the active listening game to have a voice, to make gestures and intimations yourself, and to talk with them as opposed to study, gaze, or fixate on their every action.

One of my good friends is one of the best active listeners I know, and it's no secret that he is consistently one of the top performers at a Decacorn (and recent IPO) Tech Startup. If you can master this skill, which stems from limiting your need to be important or smart, you will also see sales success.

Action Item: Test this out with a friend or colleague. In a conversation, how many times did you say what you were going to say regardless of their comments? Write it down. Where was there give and take? Improve your percentage of time that you respond to what they said as opposed to continued your speech.

4. Employs Give to Get (2 minutes)

Whenever people come over to me and ask about my sales pitch or how I approach clients, a few images come to mind. Typically, they conjure up images of me aggressively knocking down doors as if I'm on some kind of FBI most wanted crime raid. If not, they picture me with some sly, silver-tongued speech to lure people in much like the Sirens who tried to capture Odysseus. If it's not brute force or captivating charm, they think of me sitting around waiting for blue bird specials and gifts from God.

Basically, if it isn't persuasion, perspiration, or propagation, they have no idea how to be successful. So, when I start talking about how I liken myself to a doctor listening to your issues and being prescriptive in my recommendations, or a psychologist being emotionally empathetic and vulnerable, they look lost. When they ask me the one key to being successful and I respond with employing Give to Get, they look completely astonished. How is that possible? Salespeople are self-centered, how could they think about others?

If getting high off of helping others isn't for you, let me tell you why it is even in your self-interests to give first—without expectation.

Getting back to the psychologist similarity, strong sales people know the all-telling truth proved by Robert Cialdini in his book *Influence*: *Obligation trumps like.*

Think of the last time you were in a pickle trying to figure out which couple you decided to invite out; who did you choose? The ones you've known longer or the ones who just took you to dinner? The latter correct? Cialdini talks about our deep-rooted need to pay others back for the good they have done for us. So, if you go, give, gesture first—your prospects are likely to feel positive toward you when the time comes for your services. The big If here: IF your solution provided value! If you gave them—a subway passenger—a car decal, you might have missed the mark. Of course, my analogy is symbolic because while gifts are nice, they don't do much to provide initial value. Instead, you should focus your time on:

1. What clients can I introduce to their business model or cause?
2. What potential candidates do I have that could fill key positions for them?

3. What partnerships do I have that could benefit their business reach?

4. How could my company benefit from their work/word? (be careful of quid pro quo)

5. How could our companies' synergies be best served working together?

The clients/prospects that have strong matches to these five questions will be your longest and strongest relationships. To quote JFK, don't ask what your (clients) can do for you, ask what you can do for your (clients). I may have switched a couple phrases.

Action Item: Fill in these five questions for your prospect universe. Where are the synergies strongest? Spend your time with outreach to those clients/prospects.

3. Differentiates at Every Stage (2 minutes)

For those of you thinking this is a generic heading, I hear you loud and clear. It's a shame that words like "differentiate" are overused marketing buzzwords to sound smart. What I'm really getting at though is: how did you differentiate yourself? The majority of my sales experts can point to the time in the finalist meeting they really pushed apart from the pack. Some of those experts can talk about how in the demonstration they differentiated but very, very few can talk about how they differentiated in the discovery stage. Even fewer can talk about it in the prospecting or strategy stage.

The earlier and more often you can differentiate yourselves from the others, the better off you are. And, I'm not saying you should start swearing at your client to be memorable. That's not the kind of memorable you are going for. Think of the distinction between fame (good, innovative, positive association) and notoriety (bad, harmful, negative impact on society). In your pursuits, you want to build fame and distance yourself from notoriety.

What are some ways to showcase your differentiation early on? Make it personal. Not only in your outreach but in your questions too. One generic yet personal question is: what does success look like for you personally and professionally on this evaluation/engagement?

If making things personal is a challenge for you, think of how you can make your client's life easier. And no, not by implementing your product or solution.

One of my favorite ways to help make clients' lives easier is with preparing the evaluations themselves. Chances are you've helped more customers evaluate your product than they have spent time looking into buying similar solutions. You are the expert in the field so use that to THEIR advantage. Send them a sample RFP for their company to use as a guide to the evaluation. It shows you are already treating them as a client, making their life easier, and it behooves your company as the setup is likely arranged to favor your organization.

For anyone interested in further defining and developing their ability to differentiate, I highly recommend Lee Salz's aptly named book, *Sales Differentiation*.

Action Item: Evaluate your standard discovery and demonstration scripts; **are they what every other competent competitor is asking/saying?** If so, how can you stick out? Write those items down.

2. Knows What They Want, Shows Them How to Get It (Anticipate and Alleviate) (3 minutes)

I'm not one for reading autobiographies, but Stephen Schwarzman's *What it Takes* came too highly recommended for me to turn it down. I'm still reading it today, but it's interesting to see how a great pioneer like Stephen could attribute the vast majority of his success to less than a handful of events. These breaking points all hinged upon Stephen's strong brand and the relationships he built. The common bond in each of his relationships? He knew what people wanted (was confident in his abilities) and showed them how to get it. From lifting parietals at Yale to working with Japanese bankers, Stephen is one of the most vivid examples of Dale Carnegie's time-tested adage.

Recently on vacation, I read another book—*RFPs Suck!* by Tom Searcy. From an autobiography on PE to an intendedly technical way of composing winning RFPs, the principle stood tall again, further testifying to its all-encompassing presence and power. Except this time, Tom called it something else: anticipate (know what they want) and alleviate (show them how to get it).

Why is this so important? Well, it's your main value to clients. You're combining your experience with your ability to know/read them. If you don't know their concerns ahead of time, you aren't as valuable. After all, your job is to *see around corners*. They are implicitly thinking:

We want someone who's been down this track before—let us know where to bank hard, where to accelerate, when to break—**you're the driving instructor on this course**. You're the expert.

Others (subject matter experts) may know certain circuits on the course, but you're the only one who's along for every part of the ride so use that to your advantage.

If you are successful at "anticipate and alleviate," you are in fact accomplishing another important skill (you multitasker you): putting yourself in their shoes. You're saying to your client: "Yup—you're thinking this and why on earth would I do *X* when *Y* is a problem? Completely understand and here's how you can solve that problem. Here's how you mitigate *Y* so *X* can thrive."

In fact one of my best client relationships was born out of anticipating their concern. We had a strong client in other lines of business who hired a new (strong) CHRO. She was familiar with our solution line from prior organizations, and given how she was finally in place, our team thought it would be a home run. She knows us, likes us, and the organization wants us—easy! Wrong.

There was a palpable silence on the phone as we discussed our solutions. She was polite; she let us continue and thanked us for our time, but I knew something was off. I got to speak with her later that day and said: "hey, I realized you were hesitant about X, right? Coming from big companies, you probably think we are geared to the giant corporations and therefore not price-conscious of our middle-market clients like you?" I could hear her smile over the phone, and when she said "that's exactly correct, Alex"; I could feel the relief that ensued. She became a client of ours a few months down the road, and I consider her to be one of my most respected connections.

Action Item: Write your executive summaries in this Anticipate/Alleviate Framework. People appreciate real and the reality of A and A is not only entertaining, it's personal.

1. Masters the Art of Query (3 minutes)

Writing #1 on any list is a daunting task, because it's inevitably the one people will read the most intently or even skip to. Time to bust out the Morse Code you all learned in the first 99 skills for those jumping to the end.

The hardest truth we face, and it's quite nearly anyone reading this book, is that everyone likes to buy, but no one likes to be sold. The very title of salesperson gets the spidey senses going for your buyers. I mean, sales is almost half your title, and it's a dirty world. Might as well put shitty person, right? How do you turn that on its head? Well, for anyone looking for the elusive catch-all one liner, here's one to keep in mind: *If you say it, it's sold. But if they say it, it's gold.*

It's an oldie but a goodie, and it's true. Much like litigators get the witnesses to do their bidding for them, so do you. Now for anyone who read the entire book, you're going to say, how does this differ from asking effective questions? What questions you ask is important but how you ask them, when you ask; the emphasis, tone, prosody, rhythm you place on the words—makes all the difference. Asking someone what will make this project a success for them personally and professionally is a fantastic question. Provided it's at the beginning of your engagement with them. Much like asking "if it were just you deciding, would you buy? Great, does this mean you'll recommend our service to others?" Is a great question, provided it's 90 percent of the way into your sales process.

Knowing what questions to ask and when is perhaps the most valuable thing, yet no one teaches you how. So, in 250 words, how can you begin to tackle this beast? Here's a step-by-step guide:

1. Limit your situation questions, as Neil Rackham would call them; the ones you could have done in advance. These are time wasters.

2. Utilize creative questions in opening interactions; they are memorable and differentiate you. One of my favorites is aforementioned, but Jeffrey Gitomer mentions another great one: Who are your top three trusted advisors? How did they become such?

3. Start with broader, open-ended questions and then use closed questions to close or confirm.

   a. Watch how open-ended you are—are you offering pie-in-the-sky, unrealistic verbose questions? I don't have time for that.

   b. Are you asking all closed questions? Great! I can escape with one word replies and not have to lie or go into great explanations. Status quo in check!

4. Frame your questions to benefit them; end your questions with "for you," "help you," "get you" where needed.

5. Tone, prosody, pauses, emphasis are all extremely important.

   a. What are your best questions? Where should they go in the conversation and how will you get them to stop and think? As *The Challenger Sale* says, your goal should be Gee, I never thought about/considered that, hmmm…

Action Item: Come up with a word bank of your best questions for each step in the cycle. Your cold call questions, your first meeting, active pursuit/deal cycle, finalist meeting, negotiation, stalled deals, objection items, and so on. Prepare diligently beforehand. Spend 15 minutes less on mastering your product knowledge and use that time on preparing effective questions.

Thanks for reading! I hope you found some of the skills and stories very valuable to your individual endeavors and pursuits. One final thought: switch your focus from "was this good?" to "was this effective?" It shifts the conversation from subjective, in-the-past reflection to objective, forward-looking action. I wish you the best of luck and hope our paths cross. Much success to you all.

Appendix

Top 10 Books I Would Recommend Reading

In my book, you've gotten snippets of many great books—27 to be precise. You have your own proclivities to seek out those you thought most appropriate to your endeavors, and I would say to trust those instincts. The following list of 10 is ranked by how uniquely valuable, actionable, and readable I found the 27 books cited herein to be.

If you're still stuck after looking through my brief descriptions, check out my Instagram book reviews or message me at alex.dripchak@ gmail.com.

1. The Trusted Advisor

   I'm very focused on providing actionable advice, and I feel David Maister & Co. deliver checklist do's and don'ts to consultative relationships unlike anyone else. If you're able to follow their framework to a T, you are guaranteed to be successful in your professional career.

2. Sales Differentiation

   What I found particularly valuable about Lee's book is rethinking about all the items we take for granted. Most customers don't necessarily mean best, getting an RFP doesn't mean sitting around until then, not hearing back doesn't mean to follow-up relentlessly on that topic. Salz does an amazing job of getting sales people to say *The Challenger Sale's* famous line: "Huh, I never thought about it that way."

   For the playbook on what to avoid and how to pivot toward some new and innovative ideas, *Sales Differentiation* is a must read.

3. Spin Selling

   What I value most about Rackham's book is its research-oriented, scientific approach to making sales. He brilliantly distinguishes the types of sales and what types of questions and closing techniques work for each type. In a world where many either cater to one audience or take a one-size-fits-all approach, he gives you what you need to be mindful of per scenario.

Some of the key highlights include:

Making an impression in the first 2 minutes, not using closing techniques in complex, relational sales and using implication questions to move something from an inconvenience into an impactful issue that the client should take action on.

4. RFPs Suck

Of the 40+ business books I've read cover-to-cover, I'd argue that Searcy's *RFPs Suck* has the least excess. Little to no fluff in this guidebook on how to respond to RFPs and tell your most effective story. As you can imagine, it's a quick read at 120 pages; 115 of which are of differentiated value—no generic, general advice here!

5. To Sell is Human

Much like what I do here in trying to overcome the stigma and mystification of sales, Pink addresses in his book *To Sell is Human*. 80 percent of us are employing tactics and strategies to persuade, convince, negotiate, or otherwise sell ourselves in our daily professional work, so we need to understand the importance of becoming strong salespeople, overcoming the sleazy stereotypes, and focusing on success factors needed to be successful in the new buying environment.

6. The Subtle Art of Not Giving a F*ck

This book enhanced my perspective on life. It's a big statement, but it certainly carries a lot of weight.

From the backward law to what pain do you want to sustain? The book is chock full of pithy, memorable actions to improve your life. Perhaps my favorite is getting at the point that it isn't your fault for what happens to you, but it is your responsibility for how you handle it moving forward.

Mark's advice has never been more valuable and his work has been a great inspiration for my writing style.

7. What Great SalesPeople Do

The key to Michael Bosworth's *What Great SalesPeople Do* is it highlights the importance of vulnerability and empathy in connecting with others. If you "Go First," you can open up your ability to relate to your prospects and build long-lasting relationships.

8. The Relationship Edge

What's the number one most cited reason I hear about why salespeople win deals? Relationships.

In today's day and age of increasing competition and a greater number of solutions/vendors meeting core capabilities/ needs, relationships are the most effective differentiator and the wise words of one of the greatest sales professionals out there in Jerry Acuff are a great place to go to find more ways to build lifelong relationships.

9. Inked

Inked is a favorite of mine because it lays information out in a clear, consistent manner that is both engaging and effective. Blount comes back to the three principles of negotiation (leverage, power position and motivation) time and again to ensure your understanding of the topics and discusses the importance of not only tactics and strategies but emotions to be mindful of; something missing from many sales books.

10. Influence

Influence is one of the most referenced books in my book and for good reason: It's the *de facto* source on the topic of persuasion. Cialdini's textbook approach has its benefits and drawbacks. On the plus slide, it perfectly complements sales strategies with psychology, but on the downside, it can get laborious with its formal style and crammed pages (500 words on a page!).

All in all, it's still a valuable read, and in anyone's psychology or persuasion, starter pack.

Bonus: How to Win Friends & Influence People

One not listed above is the ultimate classic: *How to Win Friends & Influence People*. It's not listed because, well, I imagine most of you have already read it! This is the ideal playbook to refer to for time-tested truths, and as I like to dub its alternate title or proposed subtitle: Lessons in Likeability.

It goes beyond the confines of sales and into all daily interactions you have in life so its reach is impressive. Almost as impressive as Dale's ability to tell fascinating, engaging, and illustrious stories.

Notes

Chapter 2

1. (Dixon and Adamson 2011, pp. 60–61)

Chapter 3

1. (Calvert 2012, pp. 152–153)
2. (Blount 2020, p. 135)

Chapter 4

1. (Bosworth and Zoldan 2012, p. 142)
2. (Weinberg 2012, p. 139)

Chapter 5

1. (Acuff and Wood 2011, p. 65)

Chapter 6

1. (Manson 2016, p. 38)
2. (Manson 2016, p. 85)
3. (Salz, 2018, p. 14)

Chapter 7

1. (Gitomer 2005, p. 145)
2. (Bosworth and Zoldan 2012, p. 66)
3. (Manson 2016, p. 40)
4. (Maister, Green and Galford 2000, p. 69)
5. (Maister, Green and Galford 2000, p. 81)

Chapter 8

1. (Malhotra and Bazerman 2007, p. 61)
2. (Bosworth and Zoldan 2012, p. 126)
3. (Bosworth and Zoldan 2012, p. 54)
4. (Bosworth and Zoldan 2012, p. 47)

Chapter 9

1. (Maister, Green and Galford 2000, p. 13)
2. (Manson 2016, p. 62)
3. (Manson 2016, p. 154)

Chapter 10

1. (Konrath 2010, p. 200)

References

Acuff, J., and W. Wood. 2011. *The Relationship Edge: The Key to Strategic Influence and Selling Success*, 3rd ed. Hoboken, NJ: Wiley.

Anderson, C. 2016. *TED Talks: The Official TED Guide to Public Speaking*. Boston, MA: Mariner Books Houghton Mifflin Harcourt.

Blount, J. 2020. *Inked: The Ultimate Guide to Powerful Closing and Sales and Negotiation Tactics That Unlock Yes and Seal the Deal*. Hoboken, NJ: Wiley.

Bosworth, M., and B. Zoldan. 2012. *What Great Salespeople Do: The Science of Selling Through Emotional Connection and the Power of Story*. New York, NY: McGraw-Hill, Inc.

Calvert, D. 2012. *Discover Questions: Get You Connected*, Vol. 1, *For Professional Sellers*. Morgan Hill, CA: Winston Keen James Publishing.

Carnegie, D. 1981. *How to Win Friends and Influence People*. New York, NY: Gallery Books.

Cherry, P. 2006. *Questions That Sell: The Powerful Process for Discovering What Your Customer Really Wants*. New York, NY: AMACON.

Cialdini, R.B. 2001. *Influence: Science and Practice*, 4th ed. Needham Heights, MA: Allyn & Bacon.

Dixon, M., and B. Adamson. 2011. *The Challenger Sale: Taking Control of the Customer Conversation*. London, UK: Portfolio/Penguin.

Gitomer, J. 2005. *The Little Red Book of Selling: 12.5 Principles of Sales Greatness*. Austin, TX: Bard Press.

Grant, A. 2016. *Originals: How Non-Conformists Move the World*. New York, NY: Penguin Books.

Heiman, S.E., R.B. Miller, and Tuleja, T. 2005. *The New Strategic Selling: The Unique Sales System Proven Successful By The World's Best Companies (Revised Edition with Preface)*. New York, NY: Grand Central Publishing.

Heinecke, S. 2016. *How to Get A Meeting with Anyone: The Untapped Selling Power of Contact Marketing*. Dallas, TX: BenBella Books.

Iannarino, A. 2018. *Eat Their Lunch: Winning Customers Away From Your Competition*. London, UK: Portfolio/Penguin.

Khalsa, M. 1999. *Let's Get Real Or Let's Not Play: The Demise of Dysfunctional Selling and the Advent of Helping Clients Succeed*. Salt Lake City, UT: FranklinCovey.

Konrath, J. 2010. *Snap Selling: Speed Up Sales and Win More Business with Today's Frazzled Customers*. New York, NY: Portfolio/Penguin.

Mackay, H.B. 2005. *Swim with the Sharks Without Being Eaten Alive.* New York, NY: Harper Business.

Maister, D.H., C.H. Green, and R.M. Galford. 2000. *The Trusted Advisor.* New York, NY: Free Press.

Malhotra, D., and M.H. Bazerman. 2007. *Negotiation Genius: How to Overcome Obstacles and Achieve Brilliant Results at the Bargaining Table and Beyond.* New York, NY: Bantam Dell.

Manson, M. 2016. *The Subtle Art Of Not Giving A Fuck: A Counterintuitive Approach to Living a Good Life.* New York, NY: HarperOne.

Michalko, M. 2006. *Thinkertoys: A Handbook of Creative-Thinking Techniques,* 2nd ed. Berkeley, CA: Ten Speed Press.

Pink, D.H. 2012. *To Sell Is Human: The Surprising Truth About Moving Others.* New York, NY: Riverhead Books.

Rackham, N. 1988. *SPIN Selling.* New York, NY: McGraw-Hill, Inc.

Salz, L.B. 2018. *Sales Differentiation: 19 Powerful Strategies to Win More Deals at the Prices You Want.* New York, NY: HarperCollins Leadership.

Searcy, T. 2009. *RFPs Suck!: How to Master the RFP System Once and for All to Win Big Business.* New York, NY: Channel V Books.

Schwarzman, S. 2019. *What It Takes: Lessons in the Pursuit of Excellence.* New York, NY: Avid Reader Press/Simon & Schuster.

Sinek, S. 2009. *Start with Why: How Great Leaders Inspire Everyone to Take Action.* London, UK: Portfolio/Penguin.

Weinberg, M. 2012. *New Sales. Simplified.: The Essential Handbook for Prospecting and New Business Development.* New York, NY: AMACON.

About the Author

I am propelled forward by three deep-rooted, mind-pumping, cut-to-the-core inner monologues:

- There has to be a better way…
- How can I make a positive, lasting impact in the lives of others?
- How can I be more effective next time?

Now, on to your regularly scheduled programming.

Alex Dripchak is a Senior Advisor at Mercer, a division of Marsh & McLennan Companies. At Mercer, Alex curates and collates a solution set of over 80 specialties across six lines of business within the Total Rewards space to bring his clients resonant, repeatable, real solutions to their most critical asset: their people. In Alex's backyard of Manhattan, there are many organizations to help, but he also subspecializes in helping law firms and financial services companies.

Prior to his time at Mercer, Alex started his career at Oracle where he was an Application Sales Manager and Regional Sales Manager covering Human Capital Management Technologies. Alex was fortunate enough to be the first sales professional at Oracle to have been both a sales manager and outside producer by the age of 25.

In his quest to establish and implement that aforementioned "Better Way…" Alex has cofounded Commence, the Workforce Preparatory Academy designed to take financial, social, and professional advice and turn it into a replicable action plan to help students land their dream jobs. Through this passion project of his (and book referenced cofounder Tim Denman), Alex personalizes his 11 "power skill" program to each student to ensure they reach their maximal potential.

Message Alex @areyouworkforceready to find out his scores to the various referenced book quizzes and to keep the conversation going.

Index

CPSIA information can be obtained
at www.ICGtesting.com
Printed in the USA
BVHW050206070821
613352BV00006B/147